Comment le dire ?

- POUR S'EXPRIMER DE A À Z:
  22 FICHES D'EXPRESSIONS CLÉS
- L'ESSENTIEL DE LA GRAMMAIRE
  EN 12 POINTS

POUR S'EXPRIMER DE A À Z :
22 FICHES D'EXPRESSIONS CLÉS

ADMIRATION

That's smashing, fantastic, terrific, super!
It's really wonderful!
This is great!   **phrases exclamatives**

What a good idea!
What an interesting novel!   **What a, an + groupe nominal**

He's such a faithful friend!   **such a, an + groupe nominal**

How handsome he is!   **How + adjectif**

Isn't it nice?   **Forme interro-négative**

Well done!

I'm fascinated.

ADVICE

You should go to the doctor's.
You shouldn't speak so loud.   **should + infinitif sans to**

You ought to change your habits.   **attention : ought <u>to</u>**

You'd better hurry ; it's late.   **had better + infinitif sans to**

You could try this new medicine.

Why not buy a new car?   **Why not + infinitif sans to**

Why don't you go to the museum?

Couldn't you stop talking?

If I were you (in your position),
I wouldn't do it.

I advise you to lock the door.
I advise her not to open the door.   **proposition infinitive négative**

I suggest you attend this lecture.

What about painting your room
yourself!   **What about + V + ing**

It's (high) time you made up your
mind.   **It's time + prétérit modal**

Take my advice and go out for
a walk.   **attention : to advise (verbe),
                                      advice (nom)**

AGREEMENT

I agree with you.
I quite agree.
I agree with your opinion, your view.
   Je suis de ton (votre) avis.

I agree up to a point.
I agree to a certain extent.
   Je suis d'accord jusqu'à un certain point.

I don't entirely agree with him.

I cannot but agree with...
   Je ne peux qu'être d'accord avec...

I couldn't agree more.
   Je suis entièrement de ton avis.

I share his point of view (his opinion).
   Je partage son point de vue.

I'm of the same opinion (mind) as...
Je suis du même avis que...

She's right to believe (in believing)...

I'm perfectly ready to admit that...

I think she's right.
I think so.

How right she is! (to be right : *avoir raison*)
How true!

That's quite true!
That's a good idea.
That would be great.

I approve of his (her) going abroad.
J'approuve son départ à l'étranger.

**to approve of +
possessif + V + ing**

Yes, of course!

All right!

If you like...

Why not?

APPEARANCE

They seem to be disappointed.
It seems to me...

It appears to be easy.
It appears to me that...

I get the feeling that...
I get the impression that...

She looks lovely.
They smell bad.
It tastes delicious.
It sounds interesting.

**to look, smell, taste,
sound + adjectif**

He looks like an angel.
It smells like petrol.
It tastes like chocolate.
It sounds like classical music.

It looks, smells, tastes, sounds like + nom : *cela ressemble à, on dirait +* **nom**

She looks as if she is going to faint.

to look, smell, taste, sound + as if : *On dirait que...*

CAPACITY / INCAPACITY

He can lift this heavy weight.
She can speak Chinese.
She can't open the door.
She couldn't say a word.

can + infinitif sans to

I can't help laughing.

I can't help + V + ing

I think she'll be able to swim to the bridge.
She's unable to do it properly.
He wasn't able to ride a bike.

to be able to : équivalent de can

He managed to run away.

to manage : *réussir à*

He succeeded in repairing the TV set.

to succeed in + V + ing : *réussir à*

It's too difficult for her to stop smoking.

He knows how to repair motorbikes.
   Il sait réparer les motos.

I know I could have played better.

This computer enables me to work faster.

to enable someone to : *permettre à quelqu'un de*

It's possible for them to get the tickets.
It's quite impossible for them to get the tickets.

CAUSE

She accepted because she needed the money.
As (since) she needed money, she accepted
the job.   **as, since :** *comme, étant donné que*

That's why...
    C'est pourquoi...
That's the reason why...
    C'est la raison pour laquelle...

That accounts for his lack of energy.
    Ceci explique son manque d'énergie.

He took to drinking out of desperation.
    Il s'adonna à la boisson par désespoir.

He couldn't play football on account of his
bad health.
She couldn't take her car because of the
snow.   **on account of, because of :**
    à cause de

The bus was late due to the heavy traffic.
Owing to weather conditions the plane has
been delayed.   **due to, owing to + nom :**
    en raison de

COMPARISON

She's stronger than her friend.
He's less gifted than his brother.
    Il est moins doué que son frère.
It's more comfortable than the chair.

Her dress is as expensive as yours.
It's not so impressive as I feared.
    Ce n'est pas aussi impressionnant que je le
    craignais.

He's got as much work as you have.
They've got as many records as we have.

It's colder and colder. **de plus en plus : adjectif court**

It's more and more difficult. **de plus en plus : adjectif long**

His arguments are less and less convincing.

The more I see her, the more I love her.
Plus je la vois, plus je l'aime.
The harder he works, the better results he gets.
Plus il travaille, plus il obtient de bons résultats.

He works like a slave.

Compared to N.Y., it's warm here.
He always compares Paris with (to) New-York.

He makes a comparison with...
He bought the same record as his friend.
Our garden is similar to yours. **a comparison <u>with</u>, the same <u>as</u>, similar <u>to</u>**

He looks like his father.

COMPLAINING

I'm fed up with this job.
I'm fed up with working. **to be fed up with + nom ou gérondif :** *en avoir assez de*

Enough is enough!
I've had enough...
J'en ai assez de...

It's too much.

I'm tired of repeating the same things.
I'm tired of this mess.
I'm sick of it.
I'm sick of doing it. **to be tired of, to be sick of + nom ou gérondif**

I can't stand it any longer.
I can't stand waiting for him.
I can't bear your bad temper.
I can't bear listening to that
music.

I can't stand, I can't bear + nom ou gérondif

It drives me crazy (mad).
Cela me rend fou.

It gets on my nerves.
Cela m'énerve.

It gets on his nerves.
Cela l'énerve.

It gets on their nerves.
Cela les énerve.

What drives me crazy is queueing for hours.

What is he complaining about?
De quoi se plaint-il ?

CONDITION

If it rains, we'll stay at home.

if + présent = futur dans la principale

If it stopped raining, we'd go out.

if + prétérit = conditionnel présent dans la principale

If he had received my letter, he would have
come.

if + pluperfect = conditionnel passé dans la principale

You keep talking like this and I'll punish you.

Stop talking, otherwise you'll be
punished.

Stop talking, if not you'll be
punished.

otherwise, if not : *sinon, ou autrement*

I won't go to the party unless he apologizes.

11

You can borrow my car provided you come
back before midnight.   **provided :** *à condition que,*
                                          pourvu que

Even if I explained it to him he couldn't
understand.

Suppose he refused; what would you do?
Supposing he resigned, what would happen
to the company?

DESIRE

He wants to travel alone.

He would like to travel alone.
He'd like to travel alone.

I want him (you) to play the piano.
    Je veux qu'il (que tu) joue(s) du piano.

I'd like you to play the piano.
    J'aimerais que tu joues du piano. **I want, I'd like**
                                  + pronom personnel
                                  complément + infinitif complet

I'd love to go swimming.

I wish I had more money.
I wish you would (could) visit me more
often.   **I wish + prétérit modal**
                                          ou would, could

I'm willing to help you.

I feel like going to the theatre.   **to feel like + gérondif :** *avoir*
                                          envie de

He's longing for meeting her.   **to long for + gérondif :** *désirer*
                                          ardemment
He's dying for a decent meal.   **to die for + gérondif ou nom :**
                                          mourir d'envie de

We're looking forward to seeing
you soon.   **to look forward to + gérondif :**
                                          attendre avec impatience

12

If only you could come with us (them).

I dream of going to London.

I miss you.

DISAGREEMENT

I disagree with you.

I don't agree at all.

I don't share your point of view, your view,
your opinion.
> *Je ne partage pas votre point de vue.*

I'm sorry but I can't accept.

I'm afraid I can't agree with you.
I'm afraid I must differ with you.
I'm afraid I must express a different point
of view.

I can't admit...

I'm far from convinced that it's true.
> *Je suis loin d'être convaincu(e) que c'est
> vrai.*

I don't think she's right.
I think she's wrong.

That's not the way I see the problem.

How wrong she is!
How false!   **forme exclamative :
                              how + adjectif**

Not at all.

How could I agree with...?

I object to his coming.   **to object to + possessif +
                              gérondif :** *protester, s'élever contre*

I'm upset about that.
> *Cela me contrarie.*

I disapprove of your decision.   **to disapprove of + nom**

I disapprove of his borrowing
my car.   **to disapprove of + gérondif**

DISLIKING / LIKING

I hate getting up early.

I can't stand the rain.
I can't stand waiting in the rain.
I can't bear peeling onions.   **I can't stand, bear + nom ou gérondif**

I don't like being late.
I don't like your attitude.
I dislike your attitude.

I don't fancy this idea.
    Cette idée ne me dit rien.

I don't care for an ice-cream now.
    Je n'ai pas envie d'une glace maintenant.

I resent his telling me what to do.   **to resent + possessif + gérondif :**
    s'offusquer de, être indigné de

I can't put up with your lies.
    Je ne peux pas supporter tes mensonges.

It looks terrible.
It sounds awful.
It tastes revolting.
It smells bad.

How awful, horrible, disgusting!
It's so terrible, repulsive!
It's such a bad attitude!
What a nasty person!   **phrases exclamatives : how, so + adjectif, what a(an), such a(an) + groupe nominal**

14

The play was really terrible, bad, awful.

This smell puts me off.
Cette odeur me dégoûte.

FUTURE / INTENTION

I'll see you tomorrow.

We'll go out when he comes.
We'll go out as soon as he comes.   **présent dans la subordonnée de temps**

He's going to join us.
He's leaving at five.   **présent progressif, sens futur**

The train is about to leave.   **to be about to :** *être sur le point de*

The journalist is to meet him tomorrow.   **to be to exprime l'intention**

When will he come?

From now on I'll work harder.
A partir de maintenant (désormais), je travaillerai davantage.

They're thinking of travelling abroad.
What are you planning to do for Christmas?

He's determined to succeed.
He intends to talk to her.
They want to buy a new house.

Some day...
Un jour...
One of these days...
Un de ces jours...

GETTING SOMEONE TO DO SOMETHING

I want him (her) to...
Je veux qu'il (elle)...

I expect him to...
J'aimerais qu'il...

I'll make him repair the roof.
Have her do the shopping.   **faire faire : to have, to make someone + infinitif sans to**

Get him to do the washing-up.   **to get someone + infinitif complet**

He persuaded her to come.

He suggested we should go out. ⎤
He suggested we go out.   ⎦
     Il proposa qu'on sorte.

He forced them to open the safe.

He obliged me to give him the keys.

He convinced us to travel.

You should open the window.   **You should + infinitif sans to :**
vous devriez

Why don't you open the window?

Would you be so kind as to lend me
your book?
Would you be kind enough to lend me
your book?
     Auriez-vous la gentillesse (l'amabilité)
     de me prêter votre livre ?

Would you mind holding it
for me?   **Would you mind + gérondif**

GIVING ONE'S OPINION

From my point of view...
In my view...
In my opinion...
To my mind...
   A mon avis...

As far as I'm concerned...
   En ce qui me concerne...

I feel that...
I have the feeling that...

I believe that...
I think that...
My opinion is that...

I'm in favour of...

I'm opposed to...

We are entitled to think that...
   Nous sommes autorisés à penser que...

Speaking for myself... ⎤
As for me I think... ⎦
   Quant à moi...

I don't share the opinion...

I wonder whether (if)...
   Je me demande si...

thoughts.

At first sight I would say...
   A première vue, je dirais...
On second thoughts I would say...
   Après réflexion, je dirais...

I consider...

In fact... ⎤
Actually... ⎦
   En fait...

17

OBLIGATION

You must finish your homework.
You have to finish your homework.
You've got to finish your homework.

I am to look after my sister.　　　　**to be to :** *devoir*

I need to see you now.

Passengers are requested to remain seated.
　　Les passagers sont priés de rester assis.

It's necessary for me to have your approval.

They are requested to show their passports.
　　On leur demande de montrer leurs passeports.

He was forced to leave at once.
He was obliged to leave at once.
He was compelled to leave at once.

　　On l'obligea à partir immédiatement.

Will you stop talking!
Can't you stop talking!

Sit down!　　　　**impératif**

Do sit down!　　　　**Do : forme d'insistance**

He couldn't avoid looking at her.　**to avoid + gérondif**

PERMISSION / PROHIBITION

You can phone her now.
May I use your phone?　　　**may plus poli que can**

She's allowed to go to the disco.　**to be allowed to : équivalent de may**

Her parents allowed her to go to
the disco.

He let us play with his computer.
Il nous a laissé jouer avec son ordinateur.

You can't walk on the grass.
You're not allowed to walk on the grass.
It's forbidden to walk on the grass.
It's prohibited to walk on the grass.
It's not permitted to walk on the grass.
You mustn't walk on the grass.
Do not walk on the grass.
Il est interdit de marcher sur la pelouse.

Don't talk to me like that, will you?

No smoking.
No smoking allowed.
Interdiction de fumer.

I won't let you talk to me like that.
Je ne te laisserai pas me parler ainsi.

You aren't to use my computer.
Tu ne dois pas utiliser mon ordinateur.

You aren't supposed to use my computer.
Tu n'es pas censé utiliser mon ordinateur.

PROBABILITY /
UNCERTAINTY, CERTAINTY

It might rain.

He told me he would come but I doubt it.
... it's doubtful.

It may rain.

He may have lost my phone number.
*Il se peut qu'il ait perdu mon numéro de
téléphone.*

They can arrive before dinner.
They could arrive before dinner.

I think he has forgotten.
I presume he has forgotten.
I guess (U.S.) he has forgotten.
I suppose he has forgotten.

Perhaps he's on the way.
Maybe he's on the way.

He has probably lost my phone number.

He must be tired.
He must have lost my phone number.
> *Il a dû perdre mon numéro de téléphone.*

He should have finished by now.

I'm certain (sure) he's going to accept.

He can't have lost my phone number.

He's not likely to come again. ⎤
He's unlikely to come again. ⎦
> *Il est peu probable qu'il revienne.*

I posted it. I'm positive.
> *Je l'ai posté(e). J'en suis sûr(e).*

PROPOSING / SUGGESTING

What about a cup of tea?
What about going to an exhibition?
How about a cup of tea?
How about going to an exhibition?　**What about, how about
+ nom ou gérondif**

Would you like a cup of tea?

Shall I carry the case for you?

Let's go to the pub, shall we?
Have some fruit.　　　　**impératif**

Won't you come with us?
Will you come with us?

Why don't we go to the beach?
Why not go to the beach. **Why not + infinitif sans to**

I suggest (that) we meet earlier.

Don't you think we should meet earlier?

What would you rather have, cheese or fruit?

We could go for a walk.
We might visit the museum.

PURPOSE

He works a lot in order to succeed. ⌐
He works a lot to succeed.
He works a lot so as to succeed. ⌐

> *Il travaille beaucoup pour (afin de) réussir.*

I bought some eggs for you to make a cake.
> *J'ai acheté des œufs pour que tu fasses un gâteau.*

He switched off the radio so as not to wake them up.
> *Il éteignit la radio pour ne pas les réveiller.*

He lent her his van so that she could move out.
> *Il lui a prêté sa camionnette pour qu'elle puisse déménager.*

REFUSAL

They refused to lend us their car.

They were unwilling to lend us their car.
They were reluctant to lend us their car.
> *Ils étaient peu disposés à nous prêter leur voiture.*

They'll never agree to lend us their car.
They have no intention of lending us their
car.

It's out of the question.
I'm sorry, I can't accept this present.

No way.
Pas question, en aucune façon.
There's no reason why we should leave.
*Il n'y a aucune raison pour que nous
partions.*
I object to his doing it.
Je m'oppose à ce qu'il le fasse. **to object to + possessif + V + ing**

REPROACH

You shouldn't smoke so much.
You should have called us before.
You might have called us before.
You could have called us before.

I wish you were more polite...
J'aimerais que tu sois plus poli. **I wish + prétérit modal**

Couldn't you stop talking?
Can't you stop talking?

Why didn't you tell us the truth?

If only you had told us the truth...
Si seulement tu nous avais dit la vérité...
You ought to have told us the truth.

I'd rather you told us the truth...
*Je préférerais que tu nous dises la
vérité...* **I'd rather + prétérit modal**

I'd rather you hadn't lied to me.
*J'aurais préféré que tu ne m'aies pas
menti.* **I'd rather + pluperfect modal**

How can you speak to me like that?

How dare you speak to me like that?
Comment oses-tu me parler ainsi ?

L'ESSENTIEL DE
LA GRAMMAIRE EN 12 POINTS

1 ARTICLE DÉFINI ET INDÉFINI

◆ **Objectif** : *Savoir quand utiliser (ou omettre) l'article défini ou indéfini.*
A l'examen on peut vous demander de compléter des phrases en employant l'article défini ou indéfini quand cela est nécessaire.

AVANT DE COMMENCER...

- L'article défini s'emploie — comme son nom l'indique — devant les noms déterminés par un complément, par une subordonnée ou par le contexte.
Il ne s'emploie pas pour les généralisations.

- L'article indéfini n'a pas de pluriel.

RETENIR L'ESSENTIEL

L'article défini s'emploie pour exprimer un sens déterminé.

EMPLOI	OMISSION
• **Sens déterminé**	• **Sens général**
I like the cakes she makes.	I like cakes.
He didn't like the music of the film.	He likes music.
I don't like the blue of your wallpaper.	Blue is my favourite colour.
The love he showed was excessive.	Love is blind.
The history of Egypt is very interesting.	He studies history at University.
I can see the children. *(On parle d'enfants précis, pas d'enfants en général.)*	I can see children.

25

> *Quand le nom n'est pas déterminé, l'emploi ou l'omission de l'article défini est soumis à certaines règles.*

EMPLOI	OMISSION
Titre, grade, profession	
He interviewed the President yesterday.	● **... quand ils sont suivis du nom de la personne**
	He interviewed President Kennedy.
We saw the Queen on television.	We saw Queen Elizabeth on television.
The doctor left an hour ago.	Doctor Edwards left an hour ago.
	⚠ **Exception** : « The Emperor... » et « The Czar... » sont toujours précédés de l'article.
Noms propres	
● **Au pluriel**	● **Au singulier**
the Wilsons, the Brontës	Christ
Noms géographiques	
● **Noms de pays au pluriel**	● **Noms de pays au singulier**
the West Indies	France, England,
the British Isles	Wales *(qui est un singulier)*
⚠ **Exception** : the United Kingdom	
● **Lacs précédés de « of »**	● **Lacs**
the lake of Geneva	Lake Ontario
● **Noms de cours d'eau, d'océans et de mers**	
the Thames, the Mississippi	
the Pacific	
the Mediterranean	
● **Chaînes de montagnes**	● **Sommets**
the Alps, the Rocky Mountains	Mount Everest, Ben Nevis
● **Rues et monuments précédés de « of »**	● **Rues et monuments**
the House of Parliament	Fifth Avenue, Oxford Street, Westminster Abbey

EMPLOI	OMISSION

Noms de peuples, nationalités, langues

EMPLOI	OMISSION
• **Adjectifs substantivés** the English the French the Americans *(ensemble du peuple américain)*	English people, French people He studies English at school.

Repas, aliments, boissons

	Breakfast is ready. I don't like hamburgers. I like tea.

Matières, couleurs

	Silk is expensive. I love purple.

Périodes de temps

EMPLOI	OMISSION
• **Sens déterminé** I'll see you in the summer. *(pas l'été en général, mais l'été prochain)*	• **Sens général** I never work on Mondays. Summer is a hot season. ⚠ **Retenez bien ces expressions :** last week, next time, all night, all day long, by day, by night, at night

Inventions techniques

the telephone, the cinema, the radio	⚠ **Exception :** television

Activités humaines : jeux, sports, matières scolaires

	I play golf, chess... He studies biology.

Instruments de musique

He plays the piano and the guitar.

EMPLOI	OMISSION
Emplois commandés par la grammaire	
• **Superlatifs** the best • **Adjectifs substantivés** the rich the poor the unemployed • **Nombres ordinaux** Elizabeth the second (Elizabeth II)	• **Cas possessif** John's book • **Pronom relatif « whose »** The book whose cover is red...
I'll go to the school to meet your teachers. We must go to the hospital to visit Jane. *(emploi de l'article défini car le sens est déterminé)* ⚠ **Retenez bien ces expressions :** on the right, on the left, on the one hand, on the other hand, in the open air, in the country	⚠ **Retenez bien ces expressions :** to go to school, to church, to hospital, to market, to be at school, in jail, in prison, to go into Parliament, *(institutions : désignent l'activité plutôt que le lieu)* on earth, to go to town, hand in hand, from beginning to end, at sunrise, at sunset, body and soul, to be on time

▨▨▨ *L'article indéfini s'emploie ou s'omet dans des cas très précis. Notez ces cas particuliers d'emploi ou d'omission.*

EMPLOI	OMISSION
• **Devant un nom de métier ou de religion** His mother is an engineer. John is a catholic. • **Avec un sens distributif** twice a week, 50 pence a pound, 55 miles an hour (per hour)	• **Devant un nom au pluriel** They've got red pullovers. • **Devant un indénombrable singulier** bread, sugar, meat

<table>
<tr><td>

• **Dans les exclamations**
What a beautiful day !
Such a beautiful day !
He is so brilliant a boy !
What a pity !
What a shame !
What a mess !

• **Avec « with », « without » (attribution)**
She never goes out without a hat.

</td><td>

• **Devant la plupart des noms collectifs**
advice, news, luggage, hair, furniture
(*Mais* a piece of furniture...)

</td></tr>
</table>

Quelques pièges et difficultés

She doesn't like ~~the~~ classical music.

Sens général !
Pas d'article, même si le nom est précédé d'un adjectif !

~~The~~ Queen Elizabeth visited France yesterday.

Pas d'article pour les titres, grades, professions suivis d'un nom propre !

~~The~~ Fifth Avenue is very wide.

Pas d'article pour un nom de rue !

Come early for ~~the~~ dinner.

Pas d'article pour les repas !

Mr Simons is a ~~painter~~.

Article indéfini devant un nom de métier !

It costs 60 pence a ~~the~~ dozen.

Article indéfini pour exprimer un sens distributif !

• Ne calquez pas l'emploi de l'article défini et indéfini anglais sur le français !

2 QUEL TEMPS EMPLOYER ET POURQUOI ?

Qe

le

◆ **Objectif :** *Savoir choisir le temps qui convient en fonction de chaque phrase, de son contexte et des éléments donnés.*
A l'examen, on vous donnera le verbe à l'infinitif et on vous demandera de le mettre au temps et à la forme qui conviennent.

AVANT DE COMMENCER...

Vous devez connaître les conjugaisons à tous les temps aux formes affirmative, interrogative et négative et, en particulier, celles des verbes irréguliers.

RETENIR L'ESSENTIEL

Présent progressif

They'**re having** dinner with friends.	• **Action en train de se dérouler.**
They'**re leaving tomorrow.**	• Ce présent progressif a un **sens futur** donné par l'indicateur de temps « to morrow ».

Présent simple

She **often borrows** her father's car.	• **Action habituelle** (avec « often », « always », « never », « usually »...).
It **rains** a lot in Scotland.	• **Généralité.**
I **know** your brother.	• Certains verbes **ne s'emploient jamais à la forme progressive.** Ex. : **to know, to belong, to understand, to mean, to believe, to want, to love, to see, to like, to cost.**

I'll be a singer when I'm older.	• Présent (et **non futur**) dans une subordonnée de temps introduite par « **when** », « **as soon as** », etc. lorsque la principale est au futur.

Prétérit simple

We **saw** a very good film yesterday.	• **Action terminée, date connue.**
They **escaped** from prison three days **ago**.	• Prétérit simple avec « **ago** ».
He **studied** in Paris **for** one year when he was younger.	• **Action terminée, « for » indique la durée.**
One day I **saw** a strange man in the street, he **followed** me, I **ran** etc.	• **Temps de la narration.**

Prétérit progressif

She **was wearing** a beautiful dress.	• **Temps de la description.**
As I **was having** lunch in a restaurant, I met James.	• A l'inverse du prétérit simple, le prétérit progressif **insiste sur la durée**, le déroulement de l'action.

Prétérit modal

I wish you **were** here. If only I **could** go on holiday.	• **Souhait.**
It's (high) time you **stopped smoking**.	• Après « **it's (high) time** ».
I'd rather you **came** more often.	• Après « **I'd rather** » suivi d'un sujet différent. (Sinon, « I'd rather » est suivi d'un infinitif sans « to » : « I'd rather come ».)
If I **was** ill, I would call the doctor.	• **If + prétérit modal** avec **principale au conditionnel.**
If I were you...	• Irréalité.

Present perfect

I've **forgotten** her address.	• **Action non datée.**

She **hasn't finished** her exercises **yet**.	• Avec les adverbes tels que « ever », « never », « already », « so far », « not yet », etc.
He**'s been living** here **for** twenty years. They **have been married since** 1973.	• **Action commencée dans le passé qui se poursuit dans le présent.** « **For** » indique la durée, « **since** » le point de départ de l'action !
It's the first time I**'ve visited** this museum.	• Après « **it's the first (second...) time** ».
I'll play with you when I **have finished** my homework.	• Exprime le futur dans le passé. S'emploie lorsque la **subordonnée de temps** est **introduite par** « **after** » ou lorsque « **when** », « **as soon as** »... **ont le sens de** « **after** ».

Pour les différences entre le prétérit et le present perfect, référez-vous au chapitre suivant.

Pluperfect

When I met her she **had graduated**.	• Action antérieure à un événement passé déjà évoqué.
If I **had worked** harder, I would have passed the exam.	• **If** + **pluperfect modal** avec principale au conditionnel passé.
It was the first time she **had met** him.	• **Pluperfect modal** après « it was the first (second...) time ».

If...

If I **work** harder I**'ll succeed**.	**If** + **présent** → **principale au futur**.
If I **worked** harder, I **would succeed**.	**If** + **prétérit** → **principale au conditionnel présent**.
If I **had worked** harder, I **would have succeeded**.	**If** + **pluperfect** → **principale au conditionnel passé**.

Gérondif

It's no use crying.	• Après « **it's no use** » et d'autres expressions. (Voir chapitre sur le gérondif.)

Infinitif complet	
I **want** you **to read**. They **expected** him **to come**.	• **Après** des verbes tels que « **to want** », « **to expect** », « **to ask** », « **to prefer** », pour demander à quelqu'un de faire quelque chose par exemple.

Infinitif sans « to »	
They **mustn't leave** their cars here. **I'd rather take** a taxi.	• **Après** les **auxiliaires modaux** (attention à « ought to », voir le chapitre sur les auxiliaires modaux) et après « **I'd better** », « **I'd rather** ».

Forme passive	
The T.V. set **was repaired by** John yesterday.	• **Le sujet subit l'action.** Complément d'agent introduit par « **by** ».

Quelques pièges et difficultés

visited
I ~~have visited~~ London two years ago. *Toujours le prétérit avec « ago » !*

comes
We'll go out as soon as he ~~will come~~. *Présent dans la subordonnée de temps introduite par « as soon as » !*

have worked
I ~~work~~ here since 1989. *Action commencée dans le passé qui se poursuit dans le présent = present perfect.*

have met
It's the first time I ~~meet~~ him. *Présent perfect après « It's the first time... »*

• N'essayez pas de faire correspondre un temps français à un temps anglais.

3 PRÉTÉRIT –
PRESENT PERFECT

◆ **Objectif :** *Savoir bien utiliser les temps du passé – en particulier, bien faire la différence entre le prétérit et le present perfect – pour être capable, à l'examen, de compléter les phrases avec le temps approprié.*

AVANT DE COMMENCER...

Pour utiliser ces temps, vous devez absolument connaître par cœur les verbes irréguliers ainsi que les différences d'emploi entre « for » et « since ».

RETENIR L'ESSENTIEL

PRÉTÉRIT	PRESENT PERFECT
• **Action passée, date précisée par une indication de temps ou par le contexte.**	• **Action passée non datée. On insiste sur le résultat de cette action passée dans le présent.**
I lost my keys **yesterday**.	I have lost my keys.
We danced a lot **at Mary's wedding**.	
• **Action terminée.** **« For » indique la durée.**	• **Emploi avec « for » et « since » pour parler d'actions commencées dans le passé et qui se poursuivent dans le présent.**
He worked there **for five years** when he was younger.	She has been living here **since** 1961.
	She has been living here **for** twenty years.

PRÉTÉRIT	PRESENT PERFECT
● **Toujours le prétérit dans une phrase contenant « ago »** (action terminée). I went to Boston **three years ago.**	● **L'unité de temps à laquelle on se réfère n'est pas entièrement écoulée.** I've seen them today.
	● **Utilisation avec « ever », « never », « already », « so far », « not yet », puisque l'action a un lien avec le présent.** She has**n't** finished her exercises **yet.**
● **Le prétérit progressif exprime une action qui a une certaine durée dans le passé alors que le prétérit simple exprime un fait nouveau qui se produit.** I **was watching** T.V. **when** the telephone **rang.**	
Emplois particuliers	
● **Il arrive que le prétérit n'exprime pas le passé : on l'appelle prétérit modal.** If only I had a car ! I wish I had a car ! Would you be happy if she came ? It's (high) time you stopped smoking.	● **On emploie le present perfect avec « It's the first time ».** It's the first time I **have read** that magazine.

36

Quelques pièges et difficultés

bought
She ~~has bought~~ a book yesterday. *action passée, date connue. Prétérit.*

has lived
She ~~lived~~ here since 1981. *Present perfect si l'action se poursuit dans le présent.*

was waiting
I ~~waited~~ for the bus when I saw John. *Prétérit progressif pour exprimer une action qui a une certaine durée.*

• Ne pensez pas que le passé composé correspond systématiquement au present perfect et l'imparfait au prétérit.

Notes

4 LE PASSIF

◆ **Objectif** : *Savoir construire une phrase à la forme passive mais aussi savoir passer d'une phrase active à une phrase passive (et vice versa) comme on le demande souvent à l'examen.*

AVANT DE COMMENCER...

● La forme passive contient toujours l'auxiliaire « to be » + le participe passé du verbe à conjuguer. Il faut donc penser à réviser les participes passés irréguliers.

● « By » introduit le complément d'agent (quand il y en a un).

RETENIR L'ESSENTIEL

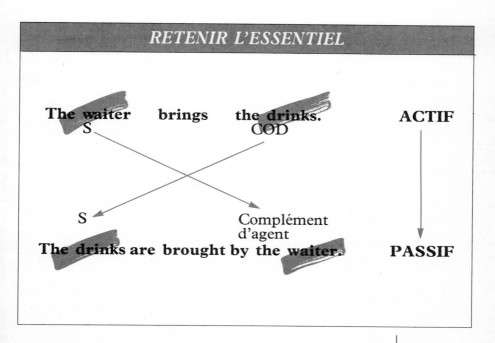

The waiter   brings   the drinks.   **ACTIF**
S   COD

S   Complément
                 d'agent
The drinks are brought by the waiter.   **PASSIF**

Les temps au passif.

Le passif peut se former à tous les temps. C'est l'auxiliaire « to be » qui indique le temps de la phrase.

ACTIF		PASSIF
The waiter **brings** the drinks.	présent	The drinks **are brought** by the waiter.
The waiter **is bringing** the drinks.	présent prog.	The drinks **are being brought** by the waiter.
The waiter **brought** the drinks.	prétérit	The drinks **were brought** by the waiter.
The waiter **was bringing** the drinks.	prétérit prog.	The drinks **were being brought** by the waiter.
The waiter **has brought** the drinks.	present perfect	The drinks **have been brought** by the waiter.
The waiter **had brought** the drinks.	pluperfect	The drinks **had been brought** by the waiter.
The waiter **will bring** the drinks.	futur	The drinks **will be brought** by the waiter.
The waiter **would bring** the drinks.	conditionnel	The drinks **would be brought** by the waiter.
The waiter **would have brought** the drinks.	cond. passé	The drinks **would have been brought** by the waiter.

L'absence de complément d'agent.

Il n'y a pas de complément d'agent quand le sujet actif est :
- un **pronom personnel**,
- **somebody, someone, no one, nobody, people**.

Ce complément d'agent n'apporterait aucun renseignement.

▰▰▰ *Cas particuliers.*

• Lorsqu'un verbe est suivi d'une **particule**, elle doit être **conservée au passif**.
The baby-sitter looked **after** the children.
The children were looked **after** by the baby-sitter.

• Le passif peut se combiner à un **auxiliaire modal**.
This medicine **can be taken** in the morning or in the evening.

• **Les verbes suivis de deux compléments d'objet direct** (to give, to tell, to offer, to teach, to lend...) ont deux constructions passives.

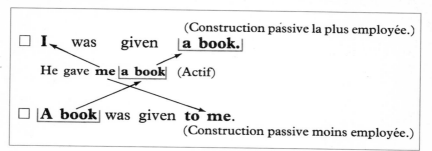

(Construction passive la plus employée.)

☐ I was given ⎢a book.⎢

He gave **me** ⎢a book⎢ (Actif)

☐ ⎢A book⎢ was given **to me**.

(Construction passive moins employée.)

• **Attention aux constructions suivantes !**

People say that he is rich.   → He is said to be rich.
People know that he is rich.   → He is known to be rich.
They told him to come earlier. → He was told to come earlier.

• Le passif est plus employé en anglais qu'en français. C'est par exemple **la traduction la plus courante de notre « on »**.

English is spoken in a lot of countries.
On *parle anglais dans beaucoup de pays.*
She is being followed. **On** *la suit.*
A bridge is being built. **On** *construit un pont.*

• **Quelques expressions passives en anglais correspondent à des expressions actives en français :**

Shakespeare was born in 1564. *Shakespeare naquit en 1564.*
She is called Calamity Jane. *Elle s'appelle Calamity Jane.*
                              On l'appelle Calamity Jane.
It's easier said than done. *C'est plus facile à dire qu'à faire.*
What is to be done ? *Que faut-il faire ?*
A few seats were left. *Il restait quelques places.*

41

Quelques pièges et difficultés

The T.V. set was repaired ~~by someone.~~ *Ne mettez de complément d'agent que s'il apporte une information !*

after

The children were looked ⌄ by the baby-sitter. *Conservez la particule au passif !*

- Souvenez-vous que le passif est beaucoup plus employé en anglais qu'en français. Certaines phrases passives en anglais se traduiront donc en français par des phrases actives !

5 LES AUXILIAIRES MODAUX :
can, could, may, might, must, shall, will, would, should, ought to...

◆ **Objectif** : *Savoir utiliser les auxiliaires modaux.*
A l'examen, on vous demandera souvent de compléter des phrases avec des auxiliaires modaux que l'on vous donne ou de terminer des phrases avec l'amorce fournie.

AVANT DE COMMENCER...

Les auxiliaires modaux permettent de modifier de multiples façons le sens d'un verbe donné en lui associant des notions telles que :

la probabilité	l'obligation	l'interdiction
la certitude	le conseil	la possibilité
l'habitude	la condition	la capacité (l'incapacité).

RETENIR L'ESSENTIEL

Caractères généraux.

• Ils ont la même forme à toutes les personnes.

• Ils se conjuguent **sans « do »** (« did ») à la forme interrogative et négative.

• Ils sont toujours **suivis de l'infinitif sans « to »**.

• Ils ne peuvent se conjuguer à tous les temps, mais ont des équivalents qui se conjuguent à tous les temps.

• Ils n'ont ni participe présent, ni participe passé.

MODAUX	EXEMPLES	SENS
CAN	He can lift this heavy table. Can you speak Italian ? Will she be able to swim that distance ?	**Capacité physique ou intellectuelle** (quelquefois traduit par « savoir »). Équivalent : **to be able to.**
	Can I go out tonight ?	**Permission.**
	Can you give me some more bread, please ?	**Demande polie.**
	He can win the championship.	**Probabilité.**
	I can hear a strange noise.	**Capacité** (devant les verbes de perception).
CAN'T	I can't visit her, I'm too busy.	**Incapacité.**
	It can't be true.	**Impossibilité.**
	You can't go out tonight.	**Interdiction.**
	I can't see him.	**Incapacité** (devant les verbes de perception).
COULD	I could dance all night when I was young.	**Prétérit de « can » (capacité dans le passé).**
	If you practised every day, you could win the tournament.	Exprime le **conditionnel.**
	Could you show me the way, please ?	**Demande polie.**
MAY	May I smoke ? She wasn't allowed to go out.	**Permission** (plus polie que « can »). Équivalent : **to be allowed to.**
	It may rain.	**Probabilité.**

MODAUX	EXEMPLES	SENS
MIGHT	The teacher said we might go out.	**Prétérit de « may » (probabilité dans le passé).**
	It might rain.	**Probabilité plus faible que « may ».**
	« What would you like to do tonight ? — We might go to the cinema. »	**Suggestion.**
MUST	You must work to earn your living.	**Obligation** (que le sujet impose à lui-même et aux autres). Équivalent : **to have to.**
	We have to go to the post-office to buy stamps.	**Obligation** (imposée par les circonstances extérieures).
	He has worked fifteen hours today, he must be tired.	**Forte probabilité.** Déduction.
	You mustn't walk on the grass. You needn't bring your camera. You don't have to do the washing-up now.	⚠ Attention à la forme négative de must. Mustn't = **interdiction.** Needn't, don't have to = **absence d'obligation.**
SHALL	Shall I open the window ?	**Suggestion** (à la forme interrogative, à la première personne du singulier et du pluriel).
WILL	Will you drive me home ? Stop talking ! Will you ?	**Invitation-demande.**
	I will open the letter.	**Volonté** (à la forme pleine accentuée).

MODAUX	EXEMPLES	SENS
WOULD	If I had money, I would travel all over the world.	Exprime le **conditionnel.**
	Would you open the window, please ?	**Requêtes polies.**
	I would like to have a computer. I would rather go to the swimming-pool.	**Désir, préférence.**
	When I was young we would often go for a picnic on Sundays.	**Action répétée dans le passé.**
SHOULD	You should stop smoking.	**Conseil** (surtout d'ordre moral, traduit en français par un conditionnel présent).
OUGHT TO	You ought to go to the doctor's.	**Conseil** (sens comparable à celui de « should »).

■■■■ *Les semi-modaux.*

Ils peuvent être employés soit comme modaux, soit comme verbes ordinaires.

SEMI-MODAUX	EXEMPLES	SENS
NEED	Need I bring more food ? You needn't come earlier.	N'a une **valeur modale qu'à la forme interrogative** pour interroger sur une obligation éventuelle **et à la forme négative.** Dans les autres cas, « need » est un verbe ordinaire.
DARE	He daren't speak in front of a large crowd.	Mêmes règles d'utilisation que pour « need ». Correspond à « oser » en français.

Quelques pièges et difficultés

I can't meeting them.   *Infinitif après l'auxiliaire modal !*

~~It is possible that he comes.~~   *He may come. → Probabilité.*

He must ~~to~~ come.   *Sauf « ought to », les auxiliaires*
She daren't ~~to~~ go out alone.   *modaux sont suivis de*
    l'infinitif sans « to ».

Shall
~~Will~~ I help you ?   *Suggestion à la première personne !*

- « Mustn't » n'exprime pas l'absence d'obligation.
Utilisez « do not have to » ou « needn't ».

- Lorsqu'on s'exprime au passé, l'auxiliaire modal ne change pas de forme, mais il est suivi d'un infinitif passé.
Observez la différence par rapport au français :

    He should have called us.
    Il aurait dû nous appeler.

Notes

47

6 LE DISCOURS INDIRECT

◆ **Objectif** : *Savoir rapporter les paroles ou les pensées de quelqu'un. A l'examen, vous aurez à mettre des phrases au style indirect (en utilisant l'amorce donnée) ou à passer du style indirect au style direct.*

AVANT DE COMMENCER...

Vous devez connaître les conjugaisons à tous les temps pour pouvoir effectuer les transformations nécessaires.

RETENIR L'ESSENTIEL

Les verbes introducteurs.

Le discours indirect peut être introduit par des verbes tels que :

to say	to think	to advise
to tell	to ask	to exclaim
to want	to offer	to command
to wonder	to order	to urge
to suggest	to request	to remind

Les pronoms personnels et adjectifs possessifs.

Le discours indirect implique généralement le **changement des pronoms personnels et adjectifs possessifs.**

La concordance des temps.

● Le discours indirect n'implique aucun changement de temps quand le verbe qui introduit les paroles rapportées est :
— au **présent**
He's tired. → He *says* (that) he's tired.
— au **futur**
She missed her train. → She *will* say (that) she missed her train.
— au **present perfect**
She will stay. → She *has said* (that) she will stay.
● Dans les autres cas, il est soumis à la règle de la **concordance des temps.**

POUR PASSER AU DISCOURS INDIRECT	
DISCOURS DIRECT (introduit par une phrase au passé)	**DISCOURS INDIRECT** (introduit par un verbe au passé)
Présent She said : « *I* **like** *your* dress. »	**Prétérit** She said (that) *she* **liked** *my* dress.
Présent progressif She said : « *I'm* **applying** for a job. »	**Prétérit progressif** She said (that) *she* **was applying** for a job.
Prétérit She said : « *I* **broke** *my* camera. »	**Pluperfect** She said (that) *she* **had broken** *her* camera.
Prétérit progressif She said : « *We* **were playing** tennis. »	**Prétérit progressif** She said (that) *they* **were playing** tennis.
Present perfect She said : « *I've* **lost** *my* glasses. »	**Pluperfect** She said (that) *she* **had lost** *her* glasses.
Futur She said : « *I'll* **marry** him. »	**Conditionnel** She said (that) *she* **would marry** him.
Conditionnel She said : « *I* **would be** glad. »	**Conditionnel** She said (that) *she* **would be** glad.

Les phrases impératives deviennent généralement des subordonnées infinitives.

He said : « Sit down ».
He asked (told...) me (him, her, us, them...) to sit down.

He said : « Don't speak ! »
He asked (told...) me (him, her, us, them...) not to speak.

Les questions.

Les **questions** qui appellent une réponse par **« yes »** ou **« no »** deviennent des **subordonnées introduites par « if » ou « whether ».**

He said : « Is he coming ? »
He asked if (whether) he was coming.

Notez le changement d'adverbes et de compléments de temps et de lieu.

DISCOURS DIRECT	DISCOURS INDIRECT
here	there
today	that day
yesterday	the day before the previous day
tomorrow	the day after the next day the following day
next month	the following month
last week	the week before
three weeks ago	three weeks before

Quelques pièges et difficultés

She said that she ~~likes~~ *liked* black coffee. *Présent → prétérit dans une phrase au passé*

Her birthday was last week and John said she would come ~~tomorrow~~ *the day after*.

N'oubliez pas de changer l'adverbe de temps !

- Commencez par regarder le temps du verbe qui introduit le style indirect. Il faut appliquer les règles de la concordance des temps seulement s'il est au passé.

- Rappelez-vous la concordance des temps :

Discours direct		Discours indirect
présent	→	prétérit
prétérit	→	pluperfect
futur	→	conditionnel
present perfect	→	pluperfect

- N'oubliez pas d'effectuer tous les changements concernant les pronoms personnels et adjectifs possessifs, les adverbes et compléments de temps et de lieu.

7 LES PHRASES EXCLAMATIVES

◆ *Objectif : Savoir exprimer une réaction émotive et connaître la grande diversité des constructions possibles.*

AVANT DE COMMENCER...

Vous devez savoir :
● reconnaître la nature des différents éléments de la phrase (adjectif, adverbe, groupe nominal ou verbe),

● distinguer sur quel élément de la phrase porte l'exclamation.

RETENIR L'ESSENTIEL

EXCLAMATION PORTANT SUR

	un adjectif ou un adverbe	un groupe nominal	un verbe
HOW	**How** expensive it was !		**How** we laughed !
SO	It was **so** expensive ! He's **so** clever a boy !		I love you **so** ! Usage remis au goût du jour par les chansons modernes. La formule plus juste serait « so much ».
WHAT		● On n'emploie l'article indéfini « a » ou « an » que lorsque « what » est suivi d'un dénombrable singulier. *Exceptions :* « What a pity, what a shame, what a mess »... **What** an idea ! **What** beautiful pictures he takes ! **What** patience he shows !	

	un adjectif ou un adverbe	un groupe nominal	un verbe
SUCH		● Pour l'emploi de l'article indéfini, mêmes règles qu'avec « what ». He's **such** an interesting man !	
SO MUCH	It was **so much** more interesting ! It was **so much** easier ! *(pour intensifier le comparatif)*	We had **so much** fun ! *(avec indénombrables seulement)*	We worked **so much** !
SO MANY		He invited **so many** friends ! *(avec dénombrables pluriel seulement)*	
SO LITTLE		She earns **so little** money ! *(avec indénombrables)*	We slept **so little** !
SO FEW		They made **so few** mistakes ! *(avec dénombrables pluriel)*	

FORME INTERRO-NÉGATIVE	Isn't she lovely ! Doesn't he look sad ! Was he happy ! La négation est parfois omise aux U.S.A.		Didn't they laugh !

Quelques pièges et difficultés

How old is he ! *N'utilisez pas l'inversion avec un mot exclamatif. Celle-ci sert à former une phrase interrogative et non une phrase exclamative !*

She isn't wonderful ! *Exclamation construite avec la forme interro-négative. Dans ce cas, faites l'inversion !*

What an interesting game ! *Attention à l'article !*

54

8 LE GÉRONDIF

◆ **Objectif :** *Vous familiariser avec cette forme très utilisée en anglais.*

● Le gérondif se forme avec la base verbale + **ing**.

● Il possède à la fois les caractéristiques d'un nom et celles d'un verbe.

RETENIR L'ESSENTIEL

▓▓▓ *Fonctions du gérondif.*

● **Sujet**
Swimming is a good exercise.

L'infinitif aussi peut être sujet :
To swim is a good exercise.

● **Complément d'objet direct**
I like swimming in the sea.

● **Complément d'objet indirect**
We talked about swimming.

▓▓▓ *Emplois du gérondif.*

● **Avec prépositions** (mais pas avec « but », ni avec le « to » de l'infinitif)

He came in without knocking at the door.
Call me before coming.
I'm fond of skiing.

⚠ Attention : après « after », le gérondif se traduira par un infinitif passé en français.
After reading she switched off the light.
Après avoir lu, elle éteignit la lumière.

They went to school after saying « goodbye ».
Ils partirent pour l'école après avoir dit « au revoir ».

● **Avec les verbes exprimant ce que l'on aime ou ce que l'on n'aime pas en général :**
to enjoy, to love, to like, to hate, to prefer...

I like travelling.
She enjoyed walking in the rain.
I hate getting up early.

⚠ Attention :
I prefer to cook now.
Je préfère faire la cuisine maintenant (dans ces circonstances).
I like cooking.
J'aime cuisiner (en général).

● **Avec les verbes exprimant le début, la fin ou la continuation d'une action :**
to start, to begin, to go on, to stop, to keep, to continue...

It started raining.
He went on working.
Stop talking, keep working.

« To start », « to begin », « to continue » peuvent être suivis d'un infinitif sans modification de sens.

⚠ Attention au verbe « to stop » :
She stopped to drink.
Elle s'arrêta pour boire.
She stopped drinking.
Elle s'arrêta de boire.

● **Avec « how about », « what about »**

How about going to the restaurant tonight?
What about going to the restaurant tonight?

● **Avec « no » exprimant l'interdiction**
No smoking!

● **Avec « to mind »**

I don't mind coming early.
Do you mind opening the window?

● **Avec les expressions**

It's no use : It's no use crying.
to be worth : This film is worth seeing.
I can't help : I can't help laughing.
to be busy : She is busy writing.

I can't bear : She can't bear peeling onions.
I can't stand : He can't stand waiting.
to spend time : She spends her time going shopping.

● **Avec « to remember »**

Gérondif et infinitif sont possibles mais **n'ont pas le même sens.**

I remember posting the letter.
Je me souviens d'avoir posté la lettre.
(gérondif = passé)
Remember to post the letter!
N'oublie pas de poster la lettre !
(infinitif = action non encore accomplie)

● **Avec « to want », « to need »...**

Notez leur sens passif lorsqu'ils sont suivis d'un gérondif.

Your hair needs cutting.
Tes cheveux ont besoin d'être coupés.

Le gérondif peut être accompagné d'un adjectif, d'un pronom personnel ou d'un cas possessif.

Do you mind his (him, John's) driving so fast?

(« him » est la variante la plus familière.)

Quelques pièges et difficultés

Don't go out without ~~to take~~ *taking* your umbrella. *Emploi du gérondif après une préposition !*

They can't help ~~to speak~~ *speaking* in class. *Emploi du gérondif après certaines expressions, dont « I can't help ».*

I like ~~to go~~ *going* to the cinema. *Gérondif pour parler de ce que l'on aime en général.*

What about ~~visit~~ *visiting* Jane. *Gérondif après « what about ».*

● Ne confondez pas :

to be used to + gérondif *(être habitué à)* ⟵
I used to + base verbale *(j'avais l'habitude de)*

9 LES SUBORDONNÉES RELATIVES

◆ **Objectif :** *Savoir construire des phrases en utilisant le bon pronom relatif, reconnaître les cas où l'omission du pronom relatif est possible.*

AVANT DE COMMENCER...

Vous devez déterminer l'antécédent du pronom relatif (le mot qu'il représente) et la fonction (sujet, complément) de ce pronom dans la subordonnée relative.

On n'emploie pas le même pronom :
● selon que l'antécédent est un être animé ou une chose,
● selon que le pronom relatif est sujet ou complément dans la subordonnée relative.

RETENIR L'ESSENTIEL

LES SUBORDONNÉES RELATIVES

FONCTION DU PRONOM RELATIF	NATURE DE L'ANTÉCÉDENT	
	ANTÉCÉDENT ANIMÉ	ANTÉCÉDENT INANIMÉ
SUJET	**WHO** The man **who** is driving is an actor. **THAT** The man **that** is driving is an actor.	**WHICH** The car **which** is parked over there is mine. **THAT** The car **that** is parked over there is mine.
COMPLÉMENT D'OBJET DIRECT	**WHOM** The girl **whom** you met yesterday is American. *(surtout langue écrite)* **THAT** The girl **that** you met yesterday is American. *(souvent employé)*	**WHICH** The book **which** he gave me was interesting. **THAT** The book **that** he gave me was very interesting. *(souvent employé)*

FONCTION DU PRONOM RELATIF	NATURE DE L'ANTÉCÉDENT	
	ANTÉCÉDENT ANIMÉ	ANTÉCÉDENT INANIMÉ
	Ø The girl **Ø** you met yesterday is American. *(très souvent employé)*	**Ø** The book **Ø** he gave me was interesting. *(très souvent employé)*
COMPLÉMENT D'OBJET INDIRECT	**PRÉP + WHOM** The man **with whom** I worked is Italian. *(surtout langue écrite)* **WHOM... PRÉP** The man **whom** you're talking **to** is a writer. *(surtout langue écrite)* **THAT... PRÉP** The girl **that** he was waiting **for** didn't come. *(souvent employé)* **Ø... PRÉP** The man they relied **on** left the country. *(très souvent employé)*	**PRÉP + WHICH** The pen **with which** I'm writing is a gift. **WHICH... PRÉP** Peter found the ball **which** I was playing **with.** **THAT... PRÉP** The chair **that** you're sitting **on** is broken. **Ø... PRÉP** He likes the pen he's writing **with.** *(plus employé à l'oral)*
COMPLÉMENT DE NOM	**WHOSE** This is the woman **whose** son is in my class. *(pas d'article après whose)*.	**WHOSE** The van **whose** doors are red is mine. *(pas d'article après whose)*. **OF WHICH** The van the doors **of which** are red is mine. *(forme peu élégante, à éviter)*

▓▓▓ *Notez également ces règles.*

● Après un superlatif et après « all », « everything », « anything », « only », on emploie **that** ou Ø.

● **La préposition accompagnant les pronoms relatifs est généralement rejetée en fin de proposition.** Le rejet est obligatoire avec **that** et Ø (**that** n'est jamais précédé d'une préposition).

The man (that) I was talking **to** was strange.

● **On ne peut employer that et Ø que lorsque la relative est déterminative** (qu'elle est indispensable à la compréhension de la phrase).

Comparez !

The students **who (that)** spoke English fluently went to London.
Les étudiants qui parlaient anglais couramment sont allés à Londres.
(Seuls ceux qui parlaient couramment sont allés à Londres. Subordonnée déterminative.)

The students, **who** spoke English fluently, went to London.
Les étudiants, qui parlaient anglais couramment, sont allés à Londres.
(Tous les étudiants parlaient anglais couramment. Ils sont allés à Londres. Subordonnée non déterminative.)

Notez l'emploi de **virgules** uniquement dans les relatives non déterminatives.

● **« What » annonce quelque chose sans antécédent.** Il s'utilise pour traduire l'idée de « ce que », « ce qui ».
What I like in this film is the music.

Les adverbes relatifs « where », « when », « why », peuvent être utilisés pour introduire une subordonnée relative.

Lieu + **« where »**	This is **the place where** I was born.
Temps + **« when »**	I remember **the day when** I met him.
Cause + **« why »**	That's **the reason why** he is late.

Quelques pièges et difficultés

The man ~~which~~ <u>who</u> came yesterday is a journalist. *Antécédent = être animé. « Who » !*

This is the best book ~~which~~ I have ever read. *Pas de « which » that ou ∅ après un superlatif !*

10 LES MOTS INTERROGATIFS

◆ **Objectif** : *Savoir utiliser le bon mot interrogatif. Un exercice couramment donné au bac consiste à trouver la question portant sur les mots soulignés.*

AVANT DE COMMENCER...

Il faut connaître la construction de la forme interrogative à tous les temps.

RETENIR L'ESSENTIEL

Sachez déduire d'une réponse donnée la question et le mot interrogatif correspondants.

Someone has stolen her bike.	→**Who** has stolen her bike ?
It depends on **their decision.**	→**What** does it depend on ?
I prefer **the red one.**	→**Which one** do you prefer ?
We'll let him know **as soon as possible.**	→**When** will we let him know ?
She'd rather go to **Scotland**.	→**Where** would she rather go ?
This car is **mine.**	→**Whose** car is it ?
He was punished **for cheating.**	→**Why** was he punished ?
His train left **at midnight**.	→**What time** did his train leave ?
I went to the chemist's **to buy some tablets.**	→**What** did you go to the chemist's **for** ?

It's very sunny today.	→ **What's** the weather **like** ?
I felt **happy** after seeing him.	→ **How** did you feel after seeing him ?
He'll be **25** next month.	→ **How old** will he be next month ?
He goes to London **twice a year.**	→ **How often** does he go to London ?
There were **hundreds of people** outside the theatre.	→ **How many** people were there outside the theatre ?
They used to pay **55 dollars** for it.	→ **How much** did they use to pay for it ?
He has been working here **for five years**.	→ **How long** has he been working here ?
It's **2 miles** from here.	→ **How far** is it from here ?
He's **5 feet 6**.	→ **How tall** is he ?
The road is **ten metres wide**.	→ **How wide** is the road ?
The swimming-pool is **2 metres deep**.	→ **How deep** is the swimming-pool ?
The parcel weighs **2 kilos**.	→ **How heavy** is the parcel ?

▬▬▬▬ *Si le pronom interrogatif est accompagné d'une préposition, celle-ci sera généralement rejetée en fin de question, après le verbe.*

He's responsible **for his little brother**.	→ **Who** is he responsible **for** ?
She likes listening **to classical music**.	→ **What** does she like listening **to** ?
They're sitting **on a bench**.	→ **What** are they sitting **on** ?

▬▬▬▬ *Notez qu'il n'y a ni inversion ni point d'interrogation dans les phrases interrogatives indirectes.*

Tell me **who you have met.**

I don't know **what he looks like.**

Ask him **why he's laughing.**

I wonder **when he arrived.**

Quelques pièges et difficultés

Who did ~~come~~ ^came^ yesterday ? *La question porte sur le sujet. On ne fait pas appel à un auxiliaire*

What time ^does^ his train ~~leaves~~ ^leave^ ? *Employez un auxiliaire pour construire la question.*

Who Lucy is calling ? *Attention à l'ordre des mots : auxiliaire + sujet + verbe.*

With what is he writing ? *Rejet de la préposition.*

Notes

11 LES PRÉPOSITIONS ET LES VERBES À PARTICULES

◆ **Objectif** : *Bien comprendre le rôle déterminant de ces petits mots appelés « particules ». Savoir quelle préposition doit accompagner un adjectif ou un verbe pour introduire un complément.*
A l'examen, on vous demandera de compléter des phrases avec la bonne préposition ou particule.

AVANT DE COMMENCER...

● Les prépositions servent à introduire un complément. Elles sont invariables.

She works **with** her cousin.
She is afraid **of** snakes.

● Les particules, associées à un verbe de base, permettent de former un nombre important de verbes composés.

RETENIR L'ESSENTIEL

▬▬ *Caractéristiques.*

Les particules font **partie intégrante du verbe** : on ne peut pas les supprimer. Elles sont en général placées **après le verbe**. Elles ne sont **pas forcément suivies d'un complément.**

She's **going up**.   He's **going down**.
Elle monte.   *Il descend.*

Ces deux exemples montrent bien que l'on peut obtenir deux verbes de sens contraire en changeant simplement la particule.

▰▰▰ *Un exemple : to look.*

to look **at**	*regarder*
to look **after**	*surveiller, s'occuper de*
to look **for**	*chercher*
to look **over**	*jeter un coup d'œil, parcourir*
to look **into**	*examiner, étudier*
to look **upon, on**	*considérer*
to look **forward to**	*attendre avec impatience*
to look **back**	*regarder derrière soi, revenir sur le passé*
to look **away**	*détourner les yeux*
to look **to**	*faire attention, veiller à*
etc.	

⚠ **Si le C.O.D. est court, on peut l'intercaler entre le verbe et la particule.**

Take **your coat** off.
Take off **your coat.**

Si le C.O.D. est un pronom personnel, vous devez obligatoirement le placer entre le verbe et la particule.
Take **it** off.

⚠ Contrairement au français, **c'est la particule** et non le verbe **qui exprime le mouvement.**
Le verbe exprime la manière dont l'action est faite.

They *swam across* the river.

mouvement — *manière*

Ils *traversèrent* la rivière *à la nage.*

Tableau des verbes composés les plus fréquents ainsi que des adjectifs et noms suivis d'une préposition.

sb : somebody. sth : something. V : verb.

ABOUT	to think about	penser à
	to speak about	parler de
	to talk about	parler de
	to worry about	s'inquiéter de
	to be crazy (mad) about	être fou de
	to be concerned about	être préoccupé de
	to be sorry about	être désolé de
AFTER	to look after	s'occuper de
AT	to look at	regarder
	to laugh at	se moquer de
	to wonder at	s'émerveiller de
	to stare at	fixer, dévisager
	to be surprised at	être surpris de
	to be good at	être bon en/à
	to be bad at	être mauvais en/à
	to be amazed at	être très étonné par
	to be angry at sth	être contrarié par
	to be amused at	être amusé par
	to be shocked at	être choqué par
FOR	to look for	chercher
	to wait for	attendre
	to send for	envoyer chercher
	to apologize for	s'excuser de
	to ask for	demander
	to exchange... for	échanger... contre
	to pay for	payer
	to long for	se languir de
	to search for	(re)chercher
	to reproach sb for sth	reprocher quelque chose à quelqu'un
	to be responsible for	être responsable de
	to be ready for	être prêt à
	to be sorry for	être désolé de
	to be useful for	être utile à
	to be prepared for sth	être préparé à quelque chose
	there is no reason for	il n'y a pas de raison de
FROM	to hear from sb	entendre parler de quelqu'un, avoir des nouvelles de quelqu'un
	to suffer from	souffrir de
	to prevent sb from + V+ing	empêcher quelqu'un de

	to keep sb from + V+ing	*interdire à quelqu'un de*
	to borrow sth from sb	*emprunter quelque chose à quelqu'un*
	to separate from	*séparer de*
	to be different from	*être différent de*
	to be absent from	*être absent de*
	to steal sth from sb	*voler quelque chose à quelqu'un*
IN	to succeed in	*réussir à*
	to be disappointed in	*être déçu par*
	to believe in	*croire en*
	to be interested in	*s'intéresser à*
	to be involved in	*être impliqué dans*
INTO	to divide into	*diviser en*
	to break into	*entrer par effraction*
	to turn (change) into	*(se) transformer en*
	to look into	*examiner*
	to run into sb	*rencontrer quelqu'un par hasard*
	to talk sb into + V+ing	*persuader quelqu'un de*
	to translate into	*traduire en*
OF	to hear of sth	*entendre parler de quelque chose*
	to think of	*penser à*
	to die of (illness)	*mourir de (maladie)*
	to approve of	*approuver*
	to disapprove of	*désapprouver*
	to remind sb of sth	*rappeler quelque chose à quelqu'un*
	to be afraid of	*avoir peur de*
	to be jealous of	*être jaloux de*
	to be ashamed of	*avoir honte de*
	to get rid of	*se débarrasser*
	to be aware (conscious) of	*être conscient de*
	to be fond of	*aimer*
	to be independent of	*être indépendant de*
OFF	to turn (switch) off	*éteindre*
	to put off	*ajourner*
	to take off	*ôter, décoller (avion)*
ON	to put on	*mettre (vêtements)*
	to depend on	*dépendre de*
	to rely on	*compter sur*
	to live on	*vivre de*
	to feed on	*(se) nourrir de*
	to spend (time) on	*passer du temps à*
	to get on well with sb	*bien s'entendre avec quelqu'un*
	to comment on	*commenter*
	to congratulate sb on	*féliciter quelqu'un de*

	to be keen on	*aimer beaucoup*
	to have mercy on	*avoir pitié de*
TO	to amount to	*s'élever à*
	to compare to	*comparer à*
	to attend to	*assister à*
	to belong to	*appartenir à*
	to listen to	*écouter*
	to prefer... to	*préférer... à*
	to look forward to + V+ing	*attendre avec impatience*
	to consent to	*consentir à*
	to be accustomed to	*être habitué à*
	to be indifferent to	*être indifférent à*
	to be prepared to + V	*être prêt à faire quelque chose*
	to be superior to	*être supérieur à*
	to be used to	*être habitué à*
	to get used to	*s'habituer à*
UP	to give up	*abandonner*
	to bring up	*élever (un enfant)*
	to look up	*chercher (dans un dictionnaire)*
	to make up	*se maquiller*
	to make up one's mind	*se décider*
WITH	to agree with sb	*être d'accord avec quelqu'un*
	to disagree with sb	*ne pas être d'accord avec quelqu'un*
	to put up with	*tolérer*
	to be fed up with	*en avoir assez de*
	to begin with	*commencer*
	to supply sth with sb	*fournir quelque chose à quelqu'un*
	to tremble with	*trembler de*
	to reproach sb with sth	*reprocher quelque chose à quelqu'un*
	to reproach sb with + V+ing	*reprocher à quelqu'un de*
	to threaten sb with sth	*menacer quelqu'un de quelque chose*
	to compare with	*comparer à*
	to deal with	*traiter de*
	to cope with	*supporter*
	to provide sb with sth	*fournir quelque chose à quelqu'un*
	to be covered with	*être recouvert de*
	to be surrounded with	*être entouré de*
	to be angry with sb	*être en colère contre quelqu'un*
	to be pleased with	*être content de*
	to be satisfied with	*être satisfait de*
	to be disappointed with	*être déçu par*

Quelques pièges et difficultés

Pick up them . *Si le C.O.D. est un pronom personnel,
il faut le placer entre le verbe et la particule !*

It depends ~~of~~ the weather. *Attention à la particule.*
    on   *Ne calquez pas sur le français !*

● Tenez compte de la particule qui accompagne le verbe de base pour bien comprendre le sens de la phrase.

12 LES MOTS DE LIAISON

◆ **Objectif** : *Savoir utiliser les mots de liaison qui conviennent pour relier deux phrases entre elles. Être capable d'opérer les transformations syntaxiques éventuelles.*
A l'examen, vous aurez soit des phrases à compléter avec le mot de liaison approprié, soit des phrases à relier entre elles en utilisant des mots de liaison.

RETENIR L'ESSENTIEL

Les mots de liaison les plus fréquents.

Vous devez les apprendre **par cœur.**

After going shopping he'll come and see us.
Après avoir fait ses courses...

Although she is rich she is not happy. *Bien qu'elle soit riche...*

As it's cloudy, I think you'd better take an umbrella.
Comme il fait gris...

As long as you don't show any fear our dog won't bite you.
Tant que tu ne manifestes aucune peur...

I'll go with you **as soon as** I've finished my letter.
... dès que j'aurai fini ma lettre.

They were not pleased **because** he had not said goodbye.
... parce qu'il n'avait pas dit au revoir.

However cold it may be she insists on going out. *Si froid qu'il fasse...*

Take your mackintosh **in case** it should start raining.
... au cas où il se mettrait à pleuvoir.

He went to England for a year **in order to** learn English.
... afin d'apprendre l'anglais.

He was a careful driver, **in spite of** that he had an accident.
... malgré cela, il eut un accident.

He went to the pictures **instead of** working. *... au lieu de travailler.*

She had **no sooner** read the letter **than** she burst into tears.
À peine eut-elle lu la lettre qu'elle fondit en larmes.

We must find a larger room **otherwise** many people will have to stay outside.
... sinon (autrement) de nombreuses personnes devront rester dehors.

You may go out tonight **provided** you come back before midnight.
... à condition que tu rentres avant minuit.

Since you are a rich man you can buy everything you want.
Puisque tu es un homme riche...

She took a taxi **so that** she might arrive on time.
... pour arriver à l'heure.

Though I have lived here for years I don't know the neighbourhood yet. *Bien que j'habite ici depuis des années...*

Wait **till** he comes. *... jusqu'à ce qu'il arrive.*

Don't answer the question **unless** you're quite sure.
... à moins que tu ne sois tout à fait sûr(e).

Unlike her husband Mrs Rod likes travelling.
Contrairement à son mari...

He will not stop shouting **until** she begins crying.
(Il criera) jusqu'à ce qu'elle se mette à pleurer.
(Il n'arrêtera pas de crier) avant qu'elle...

He never smokes **whereas** his father smokes two packets a day.
... alors que son père fume deux paquets par jour.

I wonder **whether** they'll come or not. *Je me demande s'ils viendront.*

He left the assembly **without** even saying goodbye.
... sans même dire au revoir.

■■■■■ *Exemple d'exercice (Bac 1987 - Aix-Marseille).*

En utilisant les mots de liaison suivants, reliez les deux phrases proposées en une seule, en les transformant si besoin est, mais sans en changer le sens.
(Attention : chaque mot de la liste ne doit être utilisé qu'une fois.)

whereas, while, after, since, although, instead of, in order to, on condition that

● **First he'll go shopping. Then he'll come and see us.**

Deux actions simultanées. Le mot qui peut nous permettre de relier ces phrases est « after ». Il faut supprimer « then » car il ferait double emploi. « After », comme la plupart des prépositions doit être suivi d'un gérondif pour exprimer la séquence des événements.

After going shopping he'll come and see us.
Après avoir fait les courses, il viendra nous voir.

- **You can invite him. But you must treat him well.**

On impose une condition à la personne qui voudrait faire une invitation. Il faut donc choisir « on condition that ». Le « must » contenu dans la deuxième phrase devient impossible. « On condition that » va exprimer l'obligation.

You can invite him on condition that you treat him well.
Tu peux l'inviter à condition de bien le recevoir.

- **They should have hurried. They lost time lazing around.**

Les personnes n'ont pas fait ce qu'elles auraient dû faire. Le seul mot de liaison possible est « instead of ». Il impose l'emploi du gérondif.

They should have hurried instead of losing time lazing around.
Ils auraient dû se dépêcher au lieu de perdre du temps à traîner.

- **He became a doctor. He wanted to help people.**

La deuxième phrase exprime le but. Il sera exprimé par « in order to ». Le verbe « to want » ne peut plus être employé car il ferait double emploi pour exprimer cette volonté. « In order to » doit être suivi de l'infinitif.

He became a doctor in order to help people.
Il est devenu médecin pour aider les gens.

- **He failed to keep his promise. I'll never trust him again.**

La deuxième phrase est la conséquence de la première. Il faut donc utiliser « since ». Aucune transformation syntaxique n'est nécessaire.

Since he failed to keep his promise, I'll never trust him again.
Comme il a manqué à sa promesse, je ne lui ferai plus jamais confiance.

Quelques pièges et difficultés

Do your homework instead of ~~watch~~ *watching* TV. *« Instead of » doit être suivi d'un gérondif.*

He won't come unless he is ~~not~~ invited. *Ne calquez pas sur le modèle français. Pas de négation !*

- Quand vous reliez deux phrases entre elles, pensez à opérer les changements qui s'imposent et à supprimer les mots devenus inutiles.

- Faites bien suivre les prépositions d'un gérondif.

■■■■ *Ce Q.C.M. vous propose un éventail des questions posées au bac (corrigé p. 191).*
L'essentiel est traité dans les fiches grammaticales (p. 23 à 75).
Les difficultés qui ne font pas l'objet d'une fiche sont expliquées dans la rubrique « Pour mieux comprendre » (p. 191-192).

Entourez la réponse correcte.

Vous avez un doute ?
Consultez les pages

1/ I must remember ... seats for the opera.
   a) booked
   b) booking
   c) to book
   d) I'll book

55-57 ——

2/ He would rather his friends ... tomorrow.
   a) comes
   b) has come
   c) came
   d) will come

31-34 ——

3/ We couldn't approve ... his new project.
   a) with
   b) of
   c) about
   d) in

67-72 ——

4/ Your brother can come with us to the party ... he doesn't drink all the whisky.
   a) unless
   b) otherwise
   c) yet
   d) provided

73-75 ——

5/ She can speak Russian fluently and...
   a) so does her sister
   b) her sister yes
   c) her sister doesn't
   d) so can her sister

191 ——

6/ This writer sold two ... books.
   a) million of
   b) millions
   c) million
   d) hundreds

191 ——

7/ She will not finish her work by tonight ... she starts at once.   73-75 ——
   a) unless
   b) however
   c) when

8/ This is the man ... brothers I used to work with.   59-61 ——
   a) whom
   b) whose
   c) who

9/ He read these two books but he enjoyed ... of them.   191 ——
   a) neither
   b) both
   c) either

10/ You had better start working immediately ... wasting time.   73-75 ——
   a) in spite of
   b) because of
   c) instead of

11/ She lived in England ... three months.   191 ——
   a) while
   b) for
   c) since

12/ He has done ... work since yesterday morning.   191 ——
   a) any
   b) little
   c) few

13/ My grandmother used to tell me ... marvellous stories.   53-54 ——
   a) so
   b) what
   c) such

14/ It is four years now ... he started learning English.   191 ——
   a) while
   b) when
   c) since

15/ We usually ... our holidays in a camp until last year.   35-37 ——
   a) spend
   b) are spending
   c) will spend
   d) spent

16/ She ... for half an hour when our friend came.   31-37 ——
   a) had been waiting ✓
   b) has been waiting
   c) waited
   d) was waiting

17/ I used to go to the market...   191 ——
   a) another day
   b) every other day
   c) twice
   d) the other day

18/ He had bought a novel by Fowler, but he could not tell us...   192 ——
   a) which
   b) what
   c) whatever
   d) whichever

19/ I ... be wrong but I feel sure he is not guilty.   43-47 ——
   a) should
   b) may
   c) ought to ✓
   d) can't

20/ There is ... that his T.V. show was excellent.   55-57 ——
   a) not denying
   b) not to be denied
   c) no denying
   d) not to deny

21/ You've bought far ... toys for your child.   192 ——
   a) too much
   b) many
   c) a lot of
   d) too many

22/ The Prime Minister was chosen in 1981 and has been running   192 ——
   the country...
   a) ago
   b) since when
   c) ever since
   d) from then

23/ I went to the meeting place but there was... 192 ——
   a) no one
   b) none
   c) not any
   d) no

24/ I can't find my keys, I ... left them in the kitchen. 43-47 ——
   a) would have
   b) needn't have
   c) must have ✓
   d) shall have had

25/ ... people than usual attended the concert. 192 ——
   a) So few
   b) Little
   c) Fewer
   d) So many

26/ You ... yell ; I heard you. 43-47 ——
   a) needn't
   b) ought not
   c) should
   d) may not

27/ When the phone rang ... a letter to you. 31-34 ——
   a) I wrote
   b) I should write
   c) I was writing
   d) I used to write

28/ There's hardly ... bread left. 192 ——
   a) no
   b) any
   c) much
   d) a little

29/ They show a lot of films on T.V., that's why there are ... 192 ——
spectators in the cinemas.
   a) more and more
   b) little by little
   c) so little
   d) fewer and fewer

30/ The solution will depend ... our agreement.   67-72 ——
   a) of
   b) on
   c) to
   d) from

31/ They couldn't prove ... they said.   192 ——
   a) that
   b) nothing
   c) which
   d) anything

32/ I couldn't tell one from the other ; they all looked...   192 ——
   a) like
   b) likely
   c) alike
   d) same

33/ She shouldn't believe all ... the boys say.   192 ——
   a) what
   b) that
   c) which
   d) whom

34/ I've always objected to ... my hair cut by my mother.   55-57 ——
   a) have
   b) have had
   c) having
   d) had

35/ They ... to Vienna every summer before the war.   192 ——
   a) get used
   b) are used to going
   c) used to go
   d) used to be going

36/ It won't be the first time I ... that concerto.   31-34 ——
   a) play
   b) am playing
   c) have played ✓
   d) will play

37/ He always kicks the door ...   192 ——
    a) opening
    b) open
    c) opened
    d) opens

38/ We had never eaten ... delicious pancake.   53-54 ——
    a) such
    b) so
    c) such a
    d) a such

39/ We are used to ... in the Alps.   55-57 ——
    a) go to ski
    b) go skiing
    c) going skiing
    d) go to skiing

We are used to go skiing

40/ ... strange story !   53-54 ——
    a) How
    b) What a
    c) What
    d) Which

41/ My pupils are lazy and don't care ... I say.   59-61 ——
    a) the things
    b) which
    c) what
    d) everything

42/ We said we'd play bridge while he ... the piano.   35-37 ——
    a) 'd play
    b) plays
    c) 'd played
    d) played

43/ She refuses to cook ... Sundays.   192 ——
    a) the
    b) all
    c) every
    d) on

44/ ... expensive it maybe, it's a good investment.   192 ——
   a) Though
   b) Whatever
   c) However
   d) Despite

45/ I showed her two dresses ; she didn't like ... of them.   192 ——
   a) neither
   b) all
   c) both
   d) either

46/ Haven't you ... opened the parcel which came this morning ?   192 ——
   a) ever
   b) still
   c) no longer
   d) yet

47/ He gave the beggar the ... of his two old coats.   192 ——
   a) worst
   b) worse
   c) worth
   d) worn

48/ She reproaches her children ... her.   67-72 ——
   a) to neglect
   b) should neglect
   c) neglect
   d) with neglecting

49/ I'll close the window ... you should catch a cold.   192 ——
   a) since
   b) for fear
   c) although
   d) unless

50/ I'm getting more and more impatient because I ... for ages.   31-34 ——
   a) waited
   b) have been waiting
   c) had been waiting
   d) was waiting

Civilisation

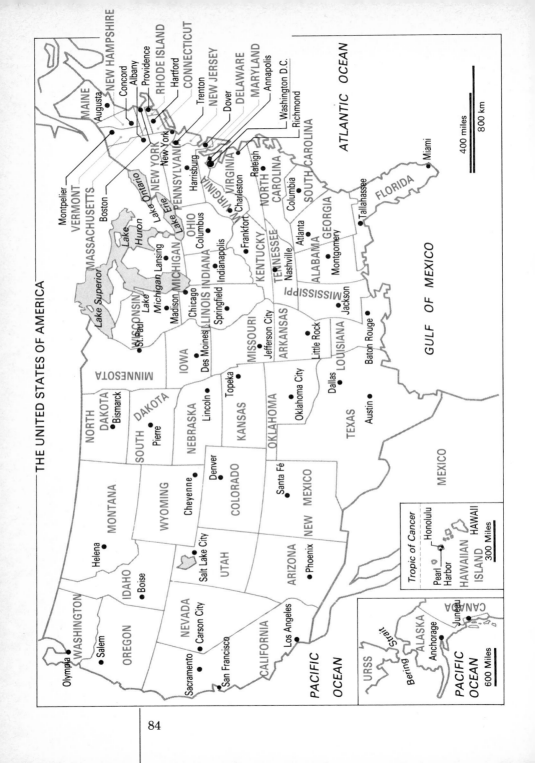

THE UNITED STATES OF AMERICA

MAINE
Augusta
NEW HAMPSHIRE
Concord
VERMONT
Montpelier
Albany
Providence
RHODE ISLAND
Hartford
CONNECTICUT
MASSACHUSETTS
Boston
NEW YORK
New York
NEW JERSEY
Trenton
DELAWARE
Dover
MARYLAND
Annapolis
Washington D.C.
Richmond
Harrisburg
PENNSYLVANIA
VIRGINIA
Raleigh
NORTH CAROLINA
SOUTH CAROLINA
Columbia
Charleston
Frankfort
KENTUCKY
Nashville
TENNESSEE
ATLANTIC OCEAN
Miami
FLORIDA
Tallahassee
GEORGIA
Atlanta
ALABAMA
Montgomery
MISSISSIPPI
Jackson
GULF OF MEXICO
Lake Ontario
Lake Erie
OHIO
Columbus
Lake Huron
Lake Superior
Lake Michigan
Lansing
MICHIGAN
WISCONSIN
St. Paul
Madison
Chicago
ILLINOIS
Springfield
INDIANA
Indianapolis
IOWA
Des Moines
MINNESOTA
NORTH DAKOTA
Bismarck
SOUTH DAKOTA
Pierre
NEBRASKA
Lincoln
MISSOURI
Jefferson City
Topeka
KANSAS
ARKANSAS
Little Rock
LOUISIANA
Baton Rouge
Oklahoma City
OKLAHOMA
Dallas
TEXAS
Austin
MEXICO
MONTANA
Helena
IDAHO
Boise
WYOMING
Cheyenne
Denver
COLORADO
Santa Fé
NEW MEXICO
Salt Lake City
UTAH
ARIZONA
Phoenix
NEVADA
Carson City
Sacramento
San Francisco
CALIFORNIA
Los Angeles
WASHINGTON
Olympia
Salem
OREGON

400 miles
800 km

Tropic of Cancer
Honolulu
Pearl Harbor
HAWAIIAN ISLAND
HAWAII
300 Miles

CANADA
URSS
Bering Strait
ALASKA
Anchorage
Juneau
PACIFIC OCEAN
600 Miles

PACIFIC OCEAN

84

1 THE COLONIAL PERIOD
THE WAR FOR INDEPENDENCE

AVANT DE COMMENCER...

The American Colonies were settled in the 17th century by Europeans, mostly English, French and Dutch.

They came to the New World for **two main reasons.**

First, for **religious and social freedom** (the Puritans, for example, fleeing religious persecution in England, settled in New England).

Secondly, for **economic freedom.** Many colonial settlers saw an opportunity to grow rich through hard work and skill in business.

These two themes, religious freedom and mercantilism, are keys to understanding the colonial experience, and contemporary America, too.

Références

Films
Dances with Wolves (Kevin Costner, 1990).
Revolution (Hugh Hudson, 1985).

VOCABULAIRE UTILE

to settle: s'installer
Dutch: Hollandais
to flee (fled, fled): fuir
opportunity: occasion
skill: compétence, habileté
brand: caractéristique, qualité
self-denial: renoncement, abnégation de soi
to set the tone: donner le ton
a settler: un colon
a crop: une culture, une récolte
to rule: gouverner
a tax: une taxe, un impôt
trade: commerce
to resent: s'offenser de
a shipment: une cargaison
to head: diriger
step: pas, étape
to occur: se produire, se passer
to surround: entourer
to surrender: se rendre

85

The Colonial Period

In 1607, English traders established the first settlement in America, and called it Jamestown, in the colony of Virginia.

The Puritans

Also known as **the Pilgrims**, they landed in the ship the *Mayflower* at **Plymouth Rock** in **Massachusetts** in **1620**. They fled England to escape religious persecution. The Puritans' brand of rigidly strict behaviour and self-denial set the tone throughout the New England colonies. Puritanism is still evident today in the American character.

Life in the colonies was extremely difficult in the early years. Fortunately, the native Americans, known as **Indians**, were friendly and helpful to the new settlers, teaching them how to grow certain crops. Their kindness was never returned, however. Within a few generations, the American Indians would become victims of what some people call a policy of genocide.

England

Throughout the mid-1700's, England ruled America with a heavy hand. The English imposed governors on the colonies, collected taxes that were often excessive and regulated trade in their own favour. The colonists resented these acts, and began to see them as interference in their own affairs. In 1773 some colonists, disguised as Indians, destroyed a shipment of British tea in Boston harbour to protest a tax on tea. This famous act of revolt, known as **"The Boston Tea Party"**, began the process that led to the **War for Independence**.

The War for Independence

The American colonies fought the war to gain their freedom from England. **During the course of the war, the thirteen original colonies declared their independence and established the United States of America.** They also wrote the **Constitution,** the fundamental laws and principles by which the country is still governed today.

The Colonial Army was headed by Gen. **George Washington.** The British Army was far better equipped and more experienced. But the Americans fought a kind of guerilla war with great fervour, since they were defending their homes and families.

1774: The **first Continental Congress** meets. Each of the thirteen colonies sends delegates to consider steps to take towards independence.

1775: The first battle of the war occurs in April, in **Lexington, Massachusetts**. Today it is referred to in American folklore as **"the Shot Heard Round The World."**

1775: **Second Continental Congress.** The Americans debate the idea of declaring independence and begin to formulate the Constitution.

1775: Famous battle of **Bunker Hill**, in **Charlestown**, near Boston. It is won by the British, but at great cost. The Americans consider it a moral victory.

1776: On **July 4th** (now celebrated as **Independence Day**), the thirteen colonies sign the **Declaration of Independence**. Its famous words have been learned by generations of American schoolchildren: "We hold these truths to be self-evident, that all men are created equal..."

1781: After several years of intermittent fighting in which neither side can gain a clear advantage, the American army, aided by the French forces, surround the British General Lord Cornwallis at **Yorktown**, Virginia, and force him to surrender. This battle ends the war.

The French played a major role in the war. Figures like **Lafayette** and **Rochambeau** fought alongside the Americans. Lafayette was decorated as an American hero after the war.

Forming a government

After the war was won, another battle remained. The new country's leaders had to persuade the colonies to accept a national, or **"federal"** government. The colonies were fiercely independent, and feared that the new federal government would be as bad as the British. But after much debate, the Federalists succeeded.

1787: The **Constitutional Convention** creates the final version of the United States Constitution.

1788: **The Constitution is ratified by the thirteen States**, and so becomes law.

1789: **George Washington is elected the first President.**

Today

Thanksgiving

The Americans still celebrate **Thanksgiving Day** in remembrance of the Pilgrim Fathers who, in 1620, thanked the Indians for their help and shared their first crop with them.

Thanksgiving is on the 4th Thursday of November. The following Friday is always a vacation day.

Thanksgiving is an important feast. Americans spend it with their families and friends, eating the famous turkey, sweet potatoes and pumpkin pies. A lot of Americans watch the Thanksgiving Parade on T.V.

The 4th of July

Every fourth (4th) of July, the Americans celebrate **Independence Day**, the birth of a new nation, in 1776, with the Declaration of Independence, which proclaimed that "all men are created equal".

The US flag

The American Flag is known as **the Star-Spangled Banner.** The 50 stars represent the 50 American states ; the 13 stripes represent the 13 original colonies which fought for American independence in 1776. *The Star-Spangled Banner* is also the title of the National anthem.

Still today you will see the American flag in many homes and front yards, specially since the Gulf war.

2 THE CIVIL WAR

AVANT DE COMMENCER...

The existence of the United States has been threatened once in its history, by the **American Civil War,** or **"the War between the States"** as it is sometimes called. The war was fought between the **North,** or the **Forces of the Union,** and the **South,** known as the **Confederates.** It left a million men dead on both sides and the South largely in ruins after the **Union Forces finally emerged victorious.**

▰▰▰ *Références*

Films
Gone With the Wind (*Autant en emporte le vent,* Victor Fleming, 1939).
Glory (Edward Zwick, 1989).
Novels
Gone With the Wind (Margaret Mitchell, 1936).

Causes

There were many causes for the Civil War, but the principal one was slavery. The **Abolitionists of the North demanded the complete elimination of slavery**. The South, largely an agrarian society whose chief crop was cotton, used slaves as its source of cheap labour. They preferred to secede from the United States and set up their own government rather than see an end to slavery.

What happened

The Civil War began in 1861 and **ended** four years later **in 1865**.

1860: **Abraham Lincoln**, the Abolitionist candidate, is narrowly elected **President**. Late the same year, the first Southern States secede from the Union.

1861: The Southern pro-slavery States form **the Confederate States of America.** Jefferson Davis is elected President of the Confederacy. The first major battle of the war is fought in July at Bull Run, and is won by the South.

1863: President Lincoln issues the **Emancipation Proclamation**, declaring that **all slaves in the United States are now free**. In November he gives the Gettysburg Address, perhaps the most famous speech by an American President. He declares that "... government of the people, by the people, and for the people shall not perish from the earth".

1864: The Southern city of Atlanta is captured by Union troops under General Sherman. This historic moment is portrayed in the film *Gone With the Wind*. General Sherman then makes his famous **"March to the Sea"**, destroying everything in his path. This campaign breaks the morale of the South. In November Lincoln is reelected President.

1865: The Civil War ends with the **surrender of Confederate General Robert E. Lee** to Union General U.S. Grant at Appomattox, Virginia. Five days later **President Lincoln is assassinated in Washington** while watching a play. His murderer, John Wilkes Booth, like many, held Lincoln responsible for the fall of the South.

The Civil War was particularly tragic for America, which had not yet survived its first century. Passions ran extremely high. Brother fought against brother, father against son. Battles were notoriously ferocious and bloody. Destruction was widespread. But the victory of the Federal forces helped to reaffirm the **country's commitment to a single union under one national government.**

Today

Today, more than one hundred years after the Civil War, the North and the South are still divided by some of the same issues that existed during the war. Racism is generally perceived to be more deep-rooted in the South, which is poorer and more conservative than the industrialized North. And many white Southerners are still proud of their Confederate past and the legends of their rebel war heroes.

Notes

3 THE GREAT DEPRESSION
ROOSEVELT'S "NEW DEAL"

AVANT DE COMMENCER...

In the '20s, America was a wild and rich country. The decade was known as **"the Roaring Twenties"**. This was the era of prohibition, when it was illegal to make or sell alcohol. But Americans drank "bootleg" liquor sold by famous gangsters like **Al Capone**.

Thousands of people became rich almost overnight, many by playing the Stock Market. But suddenly, without warning, the New York Stock Market plunged on **"Black Tuesday", October, 1929.** Millionaires were reduced to poverty, banks, businesses and factories closed, and vast numbers of Americans lost their jobs. This began **"the Great Depression"**.

Références

Films
Bonnie and Clyde (Arthur Penn, 1967).
Miller's Crossing (Joel and Ethan Coen, 1990).
The Longest Day (Darryl Zanuck, 1963).
Novels
The Grapes of Wrath (John Steinbeck, 1939).

VOCABULAIRE UTILE

the Roaring Twenties: les Années Folles
overnight: d'un jour à l'autre
the Stock Market: la Bourse
to earn a living, one's living: gagner sa vie
the drought: la sécheresse
a crop: une récolte
to chat: bavarder
to mistrust: se méfier de

93

The Move West

Out of work and with no money, many Americans **moved West**, searching for opportunities to earn a living. They camped in large settlements called **"Hoovervilles"**, ironically named after the President at the time, Herbert Hoover. In the vast farmlands of the mid-west, there was a severe drought. Farmland dried up, crops were ruined, and giant dust storms resulted. Many people, called **"Okies"** because they came from the state of **Oklahoma**, moved to California to escape their poverty.

Roosevelt's "New Deal"

In 1932, Franklin D. Roosevelt, a Democrat, was elected President. He began a program of government assistance to people in poverty, called **"the New Deal"**. He created the **Social Security system**, and started large building projects to create jobs. He spoke to the American people on the radio in his famous **"Fireside Chats"**, urging them not to lose hope. "The only thing we have to fear," he said, "is fear itself."

The War and Recovery

Slowly, the American economy recovered during the 1930's, but millions of people were still out of work. Roosevelt was **re-elected President in 1936 and 1940** (the only President in history to be re-elected more than once). But the economy did not become strong again until America began to build up its **military** in preparation for World War II. Many people found jobs in factories that manufactured war material, from guns to uniforms. In **1942**, the Japanese attacked the American naval base at **Pearl Harbor**, and **America entered the war**.

Three years later, at the end of the war, the American economy was the strongest in the world once again. Roosevelt was **re-elected for a fourth term in 1944**, but died a few months later.

Conclusion

Roosevelt's New Deal was a controversial plan. It permitted the Federal Government to intervene in the daily lives of Americans, something that the country has traditionally mistrusted. Many people criticized Roosevelt for this, but others saw him as the saviour of the country. Today he is considered one of the great Presidents of his country.

4 McCARTHYISM THE 1950's

In the years after World War II, the situation between the U.S.A. and the U.S.S.R. turned to a crisis. The hostilities between the two camps consisted in threats and violent propaganda without any direct armed conflicts. This period was called **"the cold war"**.

VOCABULAIRE UTILE

a threat: une menace
to defeat: vaincre
a stalemate: une impasse
a fake: un faux
a hearing: une audition (à un procès)
a trial: un procès
witch hunt: chasse aux sorcières
to be fired: être renvoyé
a spy: un espion
to pass a law: voter une loi
to be exposed: être démasqué, dénoncé
a liar: un menteur
to claim: prétendre
to check: vérifier
a lie: un mensonge
to be involved: être impliqué(e)

....

....

....

....

....

....

....

....

....

Références

Films
The Front (*Le Prête-Nom*, Martin Ritt, 1976).
Guilty by Suspicion (Irwin Winkler, 1990).
Plays
The Crucible (Arthur Miller, 1953).

95

The Korean War

From 1950 to 1953, the two Republics of North and South Korea, which had been created in 1948, entered the civil war.

America, along with some United Nations troops, led the effort to defeat the Communists of North Korea. It proved to be a difficult war. When Communist China sent in its own soldiers, the war ended in a stalemate. But Americans were more suspicious than ever of Communism.

The Witch Hunt

In 1950, an obscure American Senator named **Joseph McCarthy** announced that he had a secret list of 205 officials in the U.S. State Department who were members of the Communist Party (later the list was found to be a fake). The news shocked America. McCarthy held a series of televised hearings that were like court room trials.

Dozens of people were accused of being communists. Many lost their jobs and some were sent to jail, although there was often no evidence against them. Others accused their friends to save themselves. These hearings became known as the **"witch hunt", a term that comes from the Puritan era,** when witches were burned in public.

The McCarthy witch hunt extended even to **Hollywood**. People whose names were on the "black list" were accused of being communist or communist sympathizers. They were fired, or forbidden to work in the film industry. Even **Charlie Chaplin** was forced to move to England.

There was a feeling of paranoia in America during the McCarthy era. Americans thought of communism as the opposite of everything they believed in: God, individual freedom, private wealth, and the capitalist system.

There were spectacular trials: **Ethel and Julius Rosenberg** were accused of being spies for the Soviets, and they **were executed in 1953**, although the evidence against them was very questionable. A city in Alabama passed a law that made it a crime even to be seen talking to a suspected communist !

Disgrace

Finally, after four years, **Senator McCarthy was exposed as a liar**. He had built a reputation as a war hero, claiming he had flown in combat, but when his story was checked, it was found to be a lie. He later became involved in a political scandal, and was censored by the U.S. Senate in 1954. He died in disgrace in 1957.

Conclusion

The McCarthy era was known for its racism and anti-semitism as well as its anti-communism. It shows how a single demagogue can exploit the negative aspects of the Puritan spirit in the American character, such as intolerance of different beliefs and fear and suspicion of foreigners.

Notes

5 THE UNITED STATES GOVERNMENT

AVANT DE COMMENCER...

After the War for Independence was won, the first American political leaders wrote the United States Constitution. These men are known as **"the Founding Fathers"**. The Constitution has remained the fundamental document of American law and government. It states the principles of how the country is governed.

Références

Films

Mr. Smith Goes to Washington (Frank Capra, 1940).
All the President's Men (Alan Pakula, 1976).
The Candidate (Michael Ritchie, 1971).

VOCABULAIRE UTILE

to state: énoncer
to pass a law: voter une loi
to carry out the law: appliquer la loi
to initiate: prendre l'initiative de, commencer
a policy: une politique
a concern: une préoccupation
an appointment: une nomination
a justice: un juge
checks and balances: équilibre des pouvoirs
to balance: stabiliser, équilibrer
to wield power: exercer le pouvoir
to veto: mettre son veto, s'opposer à
a bill of law: un projet de loi
to impeach: révoquer
a crime: un crime, un délit
to emphasize: mettre l'accent sur
citizens' rights: les droits des citoyens
to support: soutenir

99

The structure of the United States government

The Constitution structures the government so that it consists of three branches: **the Executive, the Legislative, and the Judicial.**

The Executive Branch

The President, his Vice President, his Cabinet, and the Executive Agencies (F.B.I., C.I.A.).

The President is elected by popular vote for **a term of four years**. He can be **re-elected** for a term of four years **only once**, meaning no president can serve more than eight years. (The only exception was F. D. Roosevelt who was elected four times.) He is Commander-in-Chief of the Armed Forces. **His principal function is to see that laws passed by Congress are carried out.** The Executive Branch also initiates foreign policy.

The Legislative Branch

The Congress, consisting of the House of Representatives (the Lower House) and the Senate (the Upper House).

Congressmen are elected to the House of Representatives for **terms of two years**. There are **435 Congressmen,** and each of the fifty States has a different number of Congressmen **according to the population of that State:** California, for instance, has the greatest population, so it has the most Congressmen. The House initiates legislation and **forms government policy through the laws it passes.** Its concerns are often more local and popular in nature.

Senators are elected two **terms of six years**. There are **100 Senators**, two from each State. The Senate's concerns are generally more national and international than those of the House. It must approve all major presidential appointments, such as his Cabinet or a Supreme Court Judge. The Senate also initiates legislation.

The Judicial Branch

Local, State and Federal (National) Courts.

The Supreme Court is the highest court in America. Its rule is final on all matters of law, including the interpretation of the Constitution. There are **nine Supreme Court justices,** appointed for life by the President and confirmed by the Senate.

Checks and Balances

The American government runs according to a system of checks and balances. **The power of each branch is balanced by the other two.** Checks and balances make it impossible for any one branch of government to obtain and wield excessive power.

For example, the President can veto any bill of law created in the House or Senate. The Congress can impeach the President if he commits a crime. The Supreme Court can declare laws passed by the Congress, or actions taken by the President, to be illegal according to the Constitution. Supreme Court justices are appointed for life, but they can also be impeached by the Senate.

Through the system of checks and balances, the American people are protected from despotism in the Presidency and extremists in the Congress or the Courts.

Political parties

The President, Senators, and Representatives come from **the two major political parties: the Democratic Party and the Republican Party.**

The Democrats are the popular party. Generally, they emphasize **social equality** and believe that the Federal government should remàin strong to guarantee **citizens' rights**. They have been supported by **minorities**, especially Blacks, as well as liberal-minded groups. Recent Democratic presidents have been **Franklin D. Roosevelt, John F. Kennedy,** and **Lyndon Johnson**.

The Republicans generally support free enterprise and believe in social stability through a minimum of Federal government intervention. They tend to be the **party of the wealthy establishment**, and many of its members are **white conservatives**. Recent Republican presidents include **Dwight D. Eisenhower, Richard Nixon, Ronald Reagan** and **George Bush**.

6 IMMIGRATION

AVANT DE COMMENCER...

With the exception of the Indians, and the Blacks who were brought as slaves, America has always been **a nation of immigrants.** The Pilgrim who arrived on the *Mayflower* in 1620 was an immigrant, no less than the Mexican worker who crosses the Texas or California border today. Each came to America in search of a better life. America has been perceived as **"the land of opportunity"** for countless immigrants from every country on earth. This is **the American Dream**: the chance to succeed in life, to improve one's position both financially and socially.

▬▬ *Références*

Films
America, America (Elia Kazan, 1963).
West Side Story (Robert Wise, 1961).
The Birth of a Nation (David Griffith, 1915).

VOCABULAIRE UTILE

a border: une frontière
to flee (fled, fled): fuir
starvation: famine
a strech of land: une étendue de terre
unsettled: non peuplé
to increase: augmenter
to settle: s'installer
to compete: concurrencer
to pass a law: voter une loi
to undergo: subir
local customs: coutumes locales
to fit in: s'adapter
to give way to: faire place à
tapestry: tapisserie
hue: teinte, nuance
rags: haillons
"rags-to-riches": idée de passer de la pauvreté à la richesse
hardship: difficulté

The Three Waves

There have been **three major waves of immigration** in the history of the United States.

The First Wave began after 1800. It consisted of **the Irish**, who fled religious persecution and starvation ; **the Germans** and **Austrians** who fled war and revolution in central Europe ; and **the Scandinavians**, who also fled poverty in their native lands. For these people, America still seemed like a land of endless possibilities, with vast stretches of land unsettled in the West.

The Second Wave began about 1880. The number of new arrivals increased dramatically. They were **Catholics from southern Europe**, especially Italy and Sicily ; **Jews and Christians from central and eastern Europe**, especially Russia and Poland ; and **Asians from China and Japan.** These immigrants discovered an America that was less open. Americans began to worry about vast numbers of people settling in the crowded cities of the East Coast, competing for jobs and housing. In 1882, Congress passed a law restricting Chinese immigrants. By 1924, another law restricted immigrants of all nationalities.

The Third Wave is a phenomenon of the 1970's and 1980's. These immigrants are **Hispanics**, Spanish speaking people from Puerto Rico, Cuba, Mexico, Latin America and South America. Today they number more than **twenty million** and are the fastest growing minority in the country. They have settled mainly in California, Texas, the Southwest and Florida, but even eastern cities like New York have bilingual Spanish-English street signs and advertisements.

Also in the 1970's, **four million Asians** arrived in America. They came from Southeast Asia during and after the Vietnam War, which ended in 1975. Others came from China, Japan, the Phillipines and the Pacific Islands.

The End of the Melting Pot ?

In the early years of the twentieth century, America was known as **the Melting Pot**. The immigrants who came to America underwent a transformation, often changing their names and eagerly adopting local customs. **Their desire was "to fit in"**, to become American.

But in recent decades, this has changed. Immigrants like Asians and

Hispanics are proud of their origins. They don't want to reject their family histories. **They prefer to maintain their cultural differences.** The idea of a Melting Pot has given way to the modern reality of a rich tapestry of many hues.

The contribution of the immigrants

Immigrants have added immeasurably to the richness of American life, spiritually and materially. Americans still believe in and admire such social archetypes as **"the self-made man"**, someone who rises from poverty through initiative and hard work.

But for every **"rags-to-riches"** story, there are hundreds of other examples of immigrants whose dreams were destroyed by the harsh reality of daily life. Early in the twentieth century, a familiar saying was that "in America, the streets are paved with gold". Today's immigrants know that these same streets are often full of crime, drugs and racial discrimination.

The nature of immigration has changed, too. There are more than **five million illegal immigrants** in the U.S., the majority from Mexico. American laws make it harder to enter "the land of opportunity".

Today

Immigrants coming to America today face many of the same problems others faced a century ago, especially **racism**. But overcoming hardships like poverty and racism is also admired by Americans. They see it as part of the American Dream. Despite the many changes it has endured, **the American Dream is still alive** in the minds of millions of people of all nationalities who want to come to "the land of opportunity".

Notes

7 BLACKS

AVANT DE COMMENCER...

American Blacks are the largest minority group in America, comprising about **one-tenth of the population**. They were first brought to America as slaves in 1619, even before the Puritans arrived. For more than three centuries, Blacks have struggled to achieve equality with Whites. Although much progress has been made, American Blacks are still treated as second class citizens in many important ways.

Références

Films
Do the Right Thing (Spike Lee, 1988).
Jungle Fever (Spike Lee, 1991).
The Color Purple (Steven Spielberg, 1986).
Boyz'n the Hood (John Singleton, 1991).
Novels
Uncle Tom's Cabin (Harriet Beecher Stowe, 1852).
Nobody Knows my Name (James Baldwin, 1961).
Roots (Alex Haley, 1976).

VOCABULAIRE UTILE

a struggle: une lutte, un combat
to struggle: lutter
to achieve: atteindre
to outlaw: déclarer hors la loi, interdire
to campaign: mener campagne
to harvest: récolter, moissonner
a crop: la récolte
to secede: faire sécession, se séparer de
to free: libérer
to issue: faire paraître, proclamer
to eradicate: faire disparaître, supprimer
facilities: équipements
damaging: nuisible, préjudiciable
overt: déclaré, non déguisé
a march: un défilé, une marche
to rule: déclarer
a riot: une émeute
injured: blessé
to advocate: préconiser
to pass an act: voter une loi
a mayor: un maire
an inmate: un occupant, un détenu

107

The origins of slavery

Slavery was accepted in the early years of the United States. Even Thomas Jefferson, President and one of the founders of the nation, kept black slaves. After 1808, Congress outlawed the importation of slaves. In the North, slavery became less accepted because of the Abolitionists, people who campaigned for an end to slavery. In the South, however, slaves were used at labour to harvest the principal crops of cotton, sugar cane and tobacco.

The argument over slavery led to the **American Civil War**. The most famous anti-slavery novel, also a stage play, was Harriet Beecher Stowe's *"Uncle Tom's Cabin"*, written in 1852. When Abraham Lincoln, an Abolitionist, was elected President in 1860, eleven Southern States seceded and the war began. **In 1863, Lincoln issued the Emancipation Proclamation, freeing all the slaves.**

But in the years that followed, racism proved impossible to eradicate. In the South, violent groups like the **Ku Klux Klan** beat and lynched Blacks. They were forbidden to use white facilities, or enter white establishments like hospitals or restaurants. In the North, Blacks were forced to settle in **ghettos** in the large cities. Racism was less overt, but still damaging.

The struggle for Civil Rights

In 1909, the black leader **W.E.B. Du Bois** founded the N.A.A.C.P., **the National Association for the Advancement of Colored People.** This group forced the Supreme Court to rule in 1954 that segregation in public schools was unconstitutional. The most famous black leader was the clergyman, **Martin Luther King** (1929-1968). He organized non-violent resistance to racism, with boycotts and sit-ins. In **1963**, he led a **march on Washington** to protest racism. Hundreds of thousands of people came and heard him give his famous speech that began, "I have a dream..." **In 1964** he received **the Nobel Peace Prize**. He was **assassinated in 1968**.

In the 1960's, American Blacks reacted with violence to racism. There were riots in cities like Detroit and Los Angeles in which dozens of people were killed and thousands injured. Groups like **the Black Panthers** advocated violence as a means of self-defense.

In 1964, Congress passed the Civil Rights Act, making discrimination in public establishments and in employment illegal. **In 1965**, it passed **the Voting Rights Act**, guaranteeing Blacks the right to vote in all elections.

Today

Today, American Blacks have more legal guarantees of racial equality than ever before. America's largest cities, New York, Los Angeles, Detroit, have black mayors. The Reverend **Jesse Jackson**, a former colleague of Martin Luther King, was a presidential candidate in 1984 and 1988.

But for many Blacks, racial discrimination is as bad as ever. **More than one out of three Blacks lives below the poverty line.** One half of all black teenagers are unemployed, compared to about 7 % of white teenagers. And Blacks make up about one half of all inmates in American prisons, although Blacks represent only about one tenth of the population.

The worst aspects of American life, crime, drugs, poverty and poor education, are more prevalent among Blacks than Whites. Martin Luther King's dream of racial equality still has a long way to go before it will be achieved.

Notes

8 THE VIETNAM WAR

The Vietnam War was the most disastrous war America ever fought. It lasted ten years, **from 1965 to 1975**. More than **55,000 American soldiers died**, and **hundreds of thousands of Vietnamese were killed**. The war also caused **great damage to American society:** a whole generation of young people, and many older people, too, were opposed to the war, and they lost faith in their government and their military.

In America and throughout the world, began an **antiwar movement**. Musicians (Bob Dylan, Joan Baez), entertainers (Jane Fonda), politicians and average people too, joined the protest movement to end the war.

Vietnam was the first war that America lost.

▬▬▬ *Références*

Films
Platoon (Oliver Stone, 1986).
The Deer Hunter (*Voyage au bout de l'Enfer*, Michael Cimino, 1978).
Birdy (Alan Parker, 1984).
Good Morning Vietnam (Barry Levinson, 1988).
Born on the 4th of July (Oliver Stone, 1989).
Casualties of War (Brian De Palma, 1989).
Apocalypse Now (Francis Ford Coppola, 1979).

VOCABULAIRE UTILE

faith: foi
advisers: conseillers
to defeat: vaincre
to prove: se montrer, se révéler
to be skilled: être habile, adroit
guerilla war(fare): guérilla
to support: soutenir
the will: la volonté
costly: coûteux
to be wounded: être blessé
to withdraw: se retirer
to turn over: rendre, abandonner
to increase: augmenter
a policy: une politique
to fail: échouer
to flee (fled, fled): fuir
previous: précédent
to be addicted: s'adonner à
leadership: direction, tête
painful: douloureux

111

The early years

At the beginning of the 1960's, Vietnam was divided between South Vietnam, supported by the Americans, and North Vietnam, supported by China and the Soviet Union. **America, under President John Kennedy (elected in 1960, assassinated in 1963), sent military "advisers" to South Vietnam.** Communist forces began to attack frequently in the South. In 1965, under Lyndon Baines Johnson, the first U.S. Marines landed in Vietnam. Their job was to protect the government of South Vietnam, and help its army to defeat the communist forces operating in the South.

In these years, America believed that its military had to oppose "communist aggression" everywhere in the world.

The middle years

The war proved very soon to be a conflict between America and North Vietnam and was very hard for the American military. The communist forces, known as the **Viet Cong**, were skilled at **guerilla warfare:** they attacked at night, hid in jungles and villages and cities, and were supported by many Vietnamese civilians in the South. **The Americans** had **superior technology** and caused terrible destruction with their bombs. But, just as in the American War for Independence, the smaller force succeeded because it had the will to win and free their land from American forces.

The final years

As the war became more costly, and more Americans died or were wounded, more people opposed the war. **In 1968**, there were a **half million American soldiers fighting in Vietnam.** The same year **Richard Nixon** was elected **President**. He promised "an honorable end to the war." But the communist forces would not stop fighting until they defeated the South Vietnamese army and the Americans.

In the South, the Americans tried to withdraw and turn over the war to the South Vietnamese soldiers. In the North, the Americans increased the bombing. Both policies failed. **Finally, in 1975, the Viet Cong forces entered Saigon, the South Vietnamese capital, as the last Americans fled the city.** It was the most humiliating defeat in American history.

Today

Today many Americans believe that the Vietnam War was a horrible mistake. American soldiers were sent to a foreign country they did not understand, to fight a war they did not believe in. When they returned to the United States, they were not considered heroes, like soldiers in previous wars. Instead, Americans were suspicious of the **"Vietnam veterans"** who had been trained to kill, and some of whom were addicted to the drugs they discovered in Vietnam.

Vietnam also marked a turning point for America. The country's leadership no longer believed that the American military should intervene in any foreign country to protect democracy. **America didn't see itself as the "policeman of the free world" anymore**, and it then realized that its army, despite its advanced technology, was not invincible. The Vietnam War taught America a very painful lesson about its own limitations.

But recently the Gulf War (1991) was another turning point for America. The U.S. Army appeared as a leader of the military forces involved in the conflict. The defeat of Iraq and the victory of the allied forces deeply modified the relations between the U.S.A. and the other nations... and the relations between America and its army.

Notes

9 RELIGION

AVANT DE COMMENCER...

America was first settled by a religious group, the Puritans. Throughout history, many people have come to America to enjoy religious freedom. **Today, more than two-thirds of Americans say they belong to a specific religion**. America has always been a religious country.

Références

Films

The Rainmaker (Joseph Anthony, 1956).
The Mission (Roland Joffé, 1986).
Les Sorcières de Salem (Raymond Rouleau, 1956).

VOCABULAIRE UTILE

to be involved in: être impliqué, engagé
the homeless: les sans-abri
to interfere in: s'immiscer dans, s'ingérer dans
to support: soutenir
a poll: un sondage
abortion: avortement
to ban: interdire
to pass a law: voter une loi
network: réseau

115

How the churches function

Of the major world religions, **Protestants** make up more than **half of American churchgoers, Catholics** about **one-third** and **Jews** about **6 %**. But churches also have a social and political function in the United States. Many church groups are actively involved in community affairs, donating time and money to the poor and homeless. Some Protestant and Catholic groups are even active in foreign affairs, sending volunteers to countries like El Salvador or Nicaragua. **Churches play a direct role in social life.**

Church and State

One of the fundamental laws of the American Constitution is that **the Church and the State must always be separate:** the government must not interfere in the churches, and churches must not interfere in government. No government, state or federal, can give money to any religious group. On the other hand, the government cannot tax churches. All churches in the United States are entirely supported by private means: direct contributions from church members.

Fundamentalists and the "Born Again Christians"

According to recent polls, **one-third of Americans who are actively religious call themselves Fundamentalist Christians**. Fundamentalists are **generally conservative in politics**. They believe in the superiority of the Christian religion, and consider the word of the Bible to be absolute truth. Some members believe that in order to be "saved", they must undergo a second baptism and be "born again". Others believe it is their duty to actively convert non-believers.

Fundamentalists have recently become active in national politics. Through powerful groups like **"the Moral Majority"**, they pressure Senators and Congressmen to pass laws **against abortion and homosexuals**, and to ban school textbooks that do not teach "creationism", the theory that God literally created the world in seven days, as explained in the Bible.

The Televangelists

"Evangelists" are Christians who actively teach the Bible. "Televangelists" are Evangelists with their own **television** shows, and sometimes their own television networks. They are extremely influential and rich, with millions of daily viewers who send in

116

generous contributions. One televangelist, **Jim Bakker**, was recently sent to prison for stealing some of the millions of dollars sent to him and his wife by their Christian viewers.

Today

Religion plays a big role in American life, just as it has in past centuries. **Unlike the past, however, religion is becoming more involved in government.** No national politician can afford to ignore the religious groups today. Religious groups like the Christian Fundamentalists are adding to the return to conservative values in America: God, family and a traditional moral lifestyle.

Notes

10 THE NEWS MEDIA

AVANT DE COMMENCER...

Freedom of the press is an almost sacred right in America. It is **guaranteed by the Constitution,** and no government official, not even the President, can successfully censor the press. In fact, many politicians fear the press, which has become very powerful in the last few decades, perhaps too powerful. More than 50 % of Americans believe the news media have too much power in the United States.

▬▬▬ *Références*

Films
All the President's Men (Alan Pakula, 1976).
Citizen Kane (Orson Welles, 1941).
Broadcast News (James L. Brooks, 1987).

VOCABULAIRE UTILE

to censor: censurer
the dailies: les quotidiens
a copy: un exemplaire
coverage: ensemble des informations
the weeklies: les hebdomadaires
a topic: un sujet
to deliver: distribuer
available: disponible
a viewer: un téléspectateur
a channel: une chaîne de télévision
to devote: (se) consacrer
to broadcast: diffuser
a network: un réseau
a household: un foyer
an anchor man: un présentateur de journaux télévisés
to package: emballer
current events: actualités
one-sided: partial (d'un seul bord)

119

The Dailies

More than two-thirds of Americans read a daily paper every day. The biggest and most prestigious is the *New York Times*, which prints more than a million copies every day. The *Times* is considered the best written and most authoritative newspaper. Second to the *Times* is the *Washington Post*, which specializes in political coverage, since it is published in the nation's capital. But virtually every city and region in the United States has its own local newspaper.

The Weeklies

Weekly news magazines are also very popular. *Time Magazine* and *Newsweek Magazine* sell millions of copies each week. They specialize in news analysis and longer stories about current events. Another weekly magazine, called *People*, is extremely popular, and provides Americans with information about one of their favourite topics: celebrities.

Other magazines

There are other magazines that specialize in every imaginable topic, from television, sports and fashion to religion, handguns and car repair. Although most Americans have their newspapers and magazines delivered directly to their homes, one look in a magazine store will convince you of the incredible number and **variety of publications** available in the U.S.

Television

In the last decade, television in America has experienced an explosion in growth. Today in some metropolitan areas, it is not uncommon for viewers to have **fifty, seventy-five or even one hundred channels to choose from**.

Some channels are devoted exclusively to specific topics, like shopping, sports, weather or news, and broadcast twenty-four hours a day. Other channels broadcast in foreign languages, like Spanish or Chinese. In New York City, there is even a channel that broadcasts pornography, all day and night. Although many people disapprove of this station, the law of freedom of the press guarantees the right to broadcast.

There are three principal national networks in the U.S. that reach the largest audiences of millions of viewers: **ABC** (American Broadcasting Company), **CBS** (Columbia Broadcasting Service) and **NBC** (National Broadcasting Company).

In recent years, these have been joined by **HBO** (Home Box Office), which is the "pay TV" network that shows mostly movies, and **CNN**, the Cable News Network, that features news coverage.

Statistics show that virtually every American household has at least one T.V. set, and many have two or three. Americans watch more television than any other nationality, **between three and seven hours a day**, depending on the viewer's age and occupation.

The televised news media

Television news shows are immensely popular, and the "anchorperson" enjoys celebrity status. But these news shows also have a very strong influence on public opinion. **Nearly two-thirds of Americans learn about the news by watching television.** Therefore, public opinion is formed by what the network news shows choose to cover, or not cover, as a topic.

Some critics complain that the news shows are more interested in entertainment than in objectively reporting the news. They say that the networks have to compete for viewers, just like a television variety show, so that they tend **to "package" the news** like an attractive product that viewers can consume.

The quality of information...

Americans probably receive more information about current events than any other nationality, since there are so many different kinds of news media available, printed and televised. But many critics fear that Americans are not the best informed people because of the way some of the media present the news: often in very short segments that give a one-sided, superficial opinion of a news event. Objective, honest and intelligent reporting is too often the exception, and not the rule.

Notes

121

11 CRIME, VIOLENCE, THE HOMELESS

AVANT DE COMMENCER...

America is one of the world's most affluent nations. In spite of that, or perhaps because of it, it is also one of the most violent nations. **In 1989, more than 37 million Americans were victims of crime.** Polls show that crime and drugs are the number one concern of Americans today.

▬ *Références*

Films
Death Wish (Michael Winner, 1974).
Dirty Harry (Don Siegel, 1971).
French Connection (William Friedkin, 1971).
Taxi Driver (Martin Scorsese, 1975).
Colors (Denis Hopper, 1988).
Do the Right Thing (Spike Lee, 1988).
Jungle Fever (Spike Lee, 1991).
Boyz'n the Hood (John Singleton, 1991).
Life Stinks (Mel Brooks, 1991).

VOCABULAIRE UTILE

affluent: riche
a poll: un sondage
to claim: déclarer
on parole: (libérer) sur parole
trial: procès
income: revenu
to wander: errer

A history of crime

In the days of the Wild West, frontier towns were rough places where violence was common. Men carried guns and were quick to use them. Criminals like William Bonney, the famous **Billy the Kid,** became legendary figures, the media stars of their day.

In the 1920's, when Prohibition was in effect, organized crime brought guns and violence to the streets of American cities. Famous **bootleggers**, men who made and sold illegal alcohol, like Al Capone and Dutch Schultz, were the new legends.

Beginning in the 1960's and continuing today, illegal **drugs** have caused a new increase in crime and violence in American cities, and in suburban and rural areas, too. The 1980's saw the rise of the **street gangs** in cities like New York, Miami and Los Angeles: young, unemployed and undereducated men involved in crime and the sale of illegal drugs.

A few statistics

In 1989, nearly 650,000 men and women were in federal and state prisons in America. One newspaper article in 1990 claimed that one of every four black men between the ages of 18 and 30 is either in jail, on parole or awaiting trial. In the 1980's, the prison population of California tripled. Despite the efforts to fight criminality, violence has only increased in recent years.

Guns

America has a traditional fascination with guns that dates from the days of the Wild West. **The Constitution guarantees** that citizens have a **right to own guns**. No one knows the precise number of firearms in the United States today, because so many are obtained illegally. A powerful organization, **the National Rifle Association**, has successfully campaigned **against gun control legislation** for decades. Their success is likely to continue: President George Bush is a member.

Poverty and the Homeless

One cause for crime is poverty. **In 1990, more than 30 million Americans lived below the poverty level**, the official government statistic that measures the minimum income needed for obtaining adequate food, clothing and housing. As many as three million people are homeless, wandering the streets, searching for food and a place to sleep. In cities like New York, the contrast between fabulous wealth and crushing poverty is extreme: shiny limousines drive past men and women wrapped in blankets sleeping in doorways.

Today

Some politicians claim that crime and violence in recent years have turned some American cities into war zones. Ironically, the city with the worst violent crime problem is Washington, D.C., the nation's capital. Statistics show that there is an entire **subculture of Americans**, often poor minorities from urban areas, **involved in drugs and violent crime**. It is unquestionably the **number one problem** facing American society today.

12 AMERICAN CITIES
NEW YORK, LOS ANGELES

AVANT DE COMMENCER...

The two largest cities in the U.S. are New York and Los Angeles. Urban lifestyle in America is often very fast-paced. The cultural and economic advantages of a large American city are considerable, but so are the disadvantages.

▬▬ *Références*

Films
Colors (Dennis Hopper, 1988).
Manhattan (Woody Allen, 1979).
Taxi Driver (Martin Scorsese, 1975).
Los Angeles Stories (Mick Jackson, 1991).

VOCABULAIRE UTILE

fast-paced : d'allure rapide, accéléré
skyline: ligne d'horizon
skyscraper: gratte-ciel
to span: enjamber
borough: quartier
Stock Market: la Bourse
to be outspoken: avoir son franc-parler
bold: hardi, audacieux
the wealthy: les riches
a stockbroker: un agent de change
to step over: enjamber
to sprawl: s'étaler
per capita: par habitant
tinsel: clinquant
glittering: brillant, scintillant
movie (US): film
a drawback: un inconvénient
smog (smoke+fog): brouillard enfumé
emergency: urgence
decade: décennie
a freeway (US): une autoroute
clogged: bouché
an expense: un coût

127

New York

The first time you see the famous skyline of New York, with its huge **skyscrapers** and long bridges spanning the East River, it is an unforgettable experience.

The streets of Manhattan seem lost beneath the giant buildings. **Nine million people** live in New York City, which is divided into **five "boroughs": Manhattan, Brooklyn, Queens, the Bronx** and **Staten Island**.

New York is the **financial capital of America**, and the world, centered around the Wall Street district in Lower Manhattan, where the Stock Market is found. It is also the centre for many other activities, from publishing to theatre.

New York has many **attractions for the tourist**: the Statue of Liberty, Central Park, the theatre district at Broadway and 42nd St., the Metropolitan Museum of Art, Greenwich Village where the artists and writers have traditionally lived, Chinatown, the famous Chinese neighbourhood and much more.

New Yorkers are famous in the U.S. for their **chutzpah**, a Yiddish word meaning outspoken and bold (New York also has one of the world's largest Jewish populations).

New York is also a city of startling **contrasts**. Manhattan's Upper East Side is the exclusive district of the wealthy and powerful. Just a few kilometres away is Harlem, the famous black ghetto where many of the residents live in poverty. In the Wall Street district, homeless people sleep on the streets as millionaire stockbrokers step over them to get to work.

Life in New York can be tremendously exciting, in business and in the arts especially. But life can also be very hard there. Crime is a constant danger for all residents of all neighbourhoods. But the difficulties are part of the "legend" of New York, something most New Yorkers accept philosophically as they go about their daily business.

Los Angeles

Los Angeles is the opposite of New York in many ways. Rather than being a highly concentrated urban area with huge skyscrapers, Los Angeles is a large, **sprawling metropolitan area** with the highest per capita concentration of automobiles in the world. **More than nine million people live in the area** between the Pacific Coast and the mountains, with Los Angeles at the centre.

Los Angeles is sometimes called **"Tinsel Town"**, a city of glittering appearances. **Hollywood** lies in the heart of L.A., the movie capital of the world. The exclusive neighbourhoods of Beverly Hills and Bel Air are nearby, and a short drive south is the original Disneyland. Los Angeles, **"the City of Angels"**, is also the music capital of America.

The lifestyle in L.A. reflects that of California, generally: much more open and **"laid back"** (relaxed) than Manhattan.

But there are also drawbacks to the L.A. lifestyle. Because of its position in a valley between the ocean and the mountains, air pollution, known as **smog**, is a serious health problem. The city plans emergency measures to reduce air pollution by automobiles in the next decade. Driving in L.A. can be a nightmare: the "freeways" are often hopelessly clogged. And a recent phenomenon of violence by teenage gangs has added to the tension of living in the city. L.A., like most American cities, has its ghettos, such as the black neighbourhood of Watts.

Fascinating and frightful

The large American cities like New York, Los Angeles, Chicago, Miami, Houston, San Francisco and others, are both fascinating and frightful places to live in.

In recent years, the growing problems of crime, violence and illegal drugs, as well as the increasing expense of urban living, have made the cities less desirable than in the past.

The American urban areas are still the cultural and business centres of the country, and offer many advantages. But increasingly, the poor are excluded from these advantages, and many American cities seem sharply divided between the "haves" and the "have nots".

Notes

13 AMERICAN LIFE: FAMILY, EDUCATION AND WORK

AVANT DE COMMENCER...

The first pioneers began moving westward almost as soon as America was founded. The idea of **"moving on"**, of travelling towards a better life, is part of the American spirit even today. It is not uncommon for Americans to be born in one region of the United States, go to college in another region, take a job in another region, then move on a few years later to another region. A typical family might have relatives, such as grandparents, uncles and aunts, in several different states thousands of miles apart. **America is a very mobile society**.

▬▬▬ *Références*

Films
The Graduate (Mike Nichols, 1967).
War Games (John Badham, 1983).
Dead Poets Society (Peter Weir, 1989).
Working Girl (Mike Nichols, 1988).
Blue Collar (Paul Schrader, 1978).
Norma Rae (Martin Ritt, 1979).
Modern Times (Charlie Chaplin, 1936).

VOCABULAIRE UTILE

to found: fonder
college: université
to claim: prétendre
to break apart: se démanteler
to settle: s'installer
pace: allure
free: gratuit
compulsory: obligatoire
upon receiving: dès réception
to apply: faire une demande
graduation: diplôme de fin d'études
to support: soutenir
a standard: un niveau
to run: diriger
a degree: diplôme
a loan: un prêt
a scholarship: une bourse
fondamental to: fondamentalement lié à
to work up through the ranks (to climb up the social ladder): gravir les échelons
a failure: un « raté »
by European standards: d'après les normes européennes
vacation (US), holiday (GB): vacances
widespread: étendu
to strive: faire des efforts, lutter
to be addicted to: s'adonner à

131

The family

There is probably no "typical" American family, since America is such a complex society, made up of people of many different national origins. Sociologists have claimed that in the second half of the 20th century, the American family has begun to break apart. **The early Puritan ideal of a close family**, reinforced by immigrants in the 19th century who settled in the same cities as their relatives, **no longer exists for many Americans.**

Perhaps this is due to the rapid pace and technological advancement of much of American society. It is not unusual for an American family to watch television while grabbing a quick evening meal, or to see young children playing video games for hours on their personal computers.

There are exceptions, of course. Many Americans today are returning to the traditional values of family and religion.

Education

American children begin **Elementary School**, also called **Grade School**, at the age of 5. This education is free and compulsory until the age of 16. At the age of 12, they enter **Junior High School**, then **High School** from the age of 13 to 18.

Upon receiving their **High School Diplomas**, the certificate of graduation, students can apply to enter college. Most take the College Board Exams, called the "Scholastic Aptitude Test" (S.A.T.). A high score on this exam is necessary to enter the best colleges.

American universities are often like small cities. The concept of a college **"campus"** means that there is an entire social life at most colleges. Students live, eat and work on campus while attending classes. Many colleges have sports teams that are eagerly supported by the students when they compete against other colleges.

There are basically **two types of colleges in the U.S.** One is the **private** college: generally, these are the more expensive (as much as $20,000 per year !) and better schools. Standards are higher, it is harder to enter them, and a diploma from these schools is an advantage when starting a career. Universities such as **Harvard** in Massachusetts, **Yale** in Connecticut and **Stanford** in California are examples of the best private universities.

The other type of college is the **state** college. These are run by the different state governments. They are far less expensive, often the standards are lower and it is easier to enter them. Virtually every one of the fifty States has one or more state universities. The state university system in California has relatively high standards, and is one of the best of this type of college.

The Higher Education System		
Doctorate Degree		At least four years for a Doctorate Degree
Master's Degree	Two years for a Graduate Degree	
Bachelor's Degree in Arts or Science	Graduation	
Senior: 4th year		Four years for a Bachelor's Degree
Junior: 3rd year	Undergraduate Level	
Sophomore: 2nd year		
Freshmen: 1st year		

In recent years, competition for the highest paying jobs in America has become so intense that it is necessary to have a **Graduate Degree** even to apply for these jobs.

Americans consider a college education absolutely essential for a successful career in almost any field. Education is extremely expensive in many colleges, but most students receive government loans or scholarships from the university they attend. Even so, a typical student who graduates with a Bachelor's Degree may take 10 or even 20 years to pay back his college loans.

Although colleges such as Harvard are considered among the best in the world, there is much debate in America today about the decline in the quality of American higher education. Critics of the system fear that the average American college student is far behind European or Asian students in important areas, especially mathematics and other sciences.

Work

The American work ethic is fundamental to the American character: **that the only honest way to advance in society is through hard work.** The successful individual who begins at the bottom and "works up through the ranks" is widely admired. To be unemployed in America, regardless of the reason, is to risk being considered a failure.

It is not uncommon for Americans to ask, as soon as they meet you, what you do for work and how much money you make. The level of your salary, even more than what you do, often determines how you are seen by others.

The average workday in America begins at 8 or 9 am and ends at 5 pm. Lunch is often very short by European standards, 30 minutes or so. The average American takes only two or three weeks of vacation per year.

Like so much else in American life today, the concept of work is changing. Because of widespread computerization, some office workers and employees in technical fields **work part of the week at home** on their personal computers, which are connected to the main computers at the workplace. Many businesses encourage this practice. It keeps the employees happy and more relaxed, and helps solve the traffic problems in the cities, because less people need to drive to work each day.

Today

It is generally true that Americans strive to lead full lives. They work hard and they play hard too: they are intensive competitors. Personal pride is of great importance. The desire to succeed is very strong, and competition in most fields is very intense. This has helped to keep standards high.

But some people claim that the American attitude towards success and money is too often an obsession. This has created the phenomenon of the **"workaholic"**, someone who is addicted to work just as an alcoholic is addicted to alcohol.

Of course, most Americans are neither leaders in their fields, nor workaholics, nor unemployed. But part of the American Dream is the belief that someday, with enough hard work and a little luck, anyone can rise to the top and become a success.

134

14 CINEMA AND JAZZ

AVANT DE COMMENCER...

● **Cinema**
Hollywood is probably the best known **symbol of America,** both at home and abroad. It is a place where stars are born, dreams become reality and the poor become immensely rich. The legends of Hollywood and the great movies made there are admired throughout the world.

● **Jazz**
Jazz is a form of music that was invented in America. It came from the **music of black slaves,** or the descendants of slaves, and its early development was centered around the southern city of New Orleans in Louisiana.

▬ *Références*

Films
All that Jazz (Bob Fosse, 1979).
Around Midnight (Bertrand Tavernier, 1986).
Sunset Boulevard (Billy Wilder, 1950).
Frances (Graeme Clifford, 1983).
Bird (Clint Eastwood, 1987).
Let's get lost (Bruce Weber, 1988).
Barton Fink (Joel and Ethan Coen, 1991).
Cotton Club (Francis Ford Coppola, 1984).

VOCABULAIRE UTILE

a movie (US), a film (GB): un film
a sound track: une bande-son
a talkie: un film parlant
a director: un metteur en scène
proficient: compétent
an alternative: une possibilité
self-taught: autodidacte

135

CINEMA

The Silent era

The American film industry began in the late 19th century. The era of **silent films** had its own stars in the early years of the 20th century. Silent comedy was particularly well loved. Stars such as **Charlie Chaplin**, **Buster Keaton** and **Harol Lloyd** made millions of people laugh.

The Golden era

The Jazz Singer starring Al Jolson **in 1927** was the **first major "talkie"**, or movie with a sound track, and it created a sensation. In Hollywood, the powerful Film Studios were established, and competed with each other for the big stars and famous directors. During the Great Depression in the 1930's, Americans turned to movies as a way of forgetting their problems.

In the 1940's and 1950's, many excellent European directors came to Hollywood to escape the effects of the war. They were also tempted by the huge salaries paid to the Hollywood stars. This period saw great actors such as Humphrey Bogart, James Stewart, James Dean, Marlon Brando, Jean Harlow, Rita Hayworth, Marilyn Monroe and many others. In 1946, the first year after the war ended, more people than ever before went to the movies in America. But the following year, television was introduced, and Hollywood's Golden era was coming to an end.

The Television era

As television became more popular, fewer people paid to go to the movies. But the film studios soon formed their own T.V. production studios. Today Hollywood is also the centre of the American television industry.

Today

The American film industry remains the world's largest and most technically proficient. But many younger independent American filmmakers turn elsewhere to make their movies. Hollywood is no longer the only alternative for directors and actors. Some filmmakers complain that film industry is too interested in making money, and doesn't care enough about quality.

Films today can easily cost 10 or 20 million dollars to make, but successful films, called "box office hits" or "blockbusters" can make hundreds of millions of dollars in profit. Private investors, often business people who know nothing about filmmaking, are sought to provide the money to make a film, and they expect to make a large profit. In the later part of the 20th century, film industry has become more like a giant corporation.

JAZZ

Jazz relies on **improvisation,** and less on theory, although it requires great technical skill. This is why it was so popular with black American musicians, many of whom were self-taught and very talented, but had little formal training in music. Ironically, jazz had a strong influence on some great European composers, such as Igor Stravinsky.

After its birth in the South, jazz moved to the northern cities with the Blacks who sought better jobs and less restrictions on their personal freedom. Jazz clubs were popular in New York's Harlem district, as well as in Chicago in the 1930's and after. In the 1920's, American jazz musicians came to Europe, where they were very popular in cities like Paris, London and Berlin.

Some of the great American jazz musicians of the past are legends: Louis Armstrong, called "Satchmo", Ella Fitzgerald, Charlie Parker, John Coltrane, Duke Ellington, Billie Holliday.

Although never as popular as rock, jazz still has a large number of fans, and they follow their favourite music with religious devotion. Jazz has a very special place in the history of America, for it is one of the few totally American art forms.

In the recent years, jazz has been influenced by more varied forms of music. Blues is no longer the dominating musical influence. Among modern jazzmen, there are Stan Getz, Charlie Mingus, Art Pepper, Herbie Hancock, Keith Jarrett, Miles Davis...

Notes

137

THE UNITED KINGDOM

North

West — East

South

ATLANTIC

OCEAN

Orkney Islands

Shetland Islands

Aberdeen

SCOTLAND

Dundee

NORTH   SEA

Glasgow

Edinburgh

Tweed

North Channel

Tyne

Newcastle

NORTHERN IRELAND
(Ulster)

Belfast

Carlisle

Isle of Man

York

IRISH SEA

Leeds

Manchester

Liverpool

Sheffield

Trent

DUBLIN

REPUBLIC
OF
(Eire) IRELAND

Shannon

Nottingham

Norwich

Birmingham

Severn

Coventry

Cambridge

St George's Channel

Worcester

Gloucester

WALES

ENGLAND

Oxford

LONDON

Canterbury

Cardiff

Bristol

Thames

Dover

Bristol Channel

Hastings

Southampton

Brighton

Strait of Dover

Plymouth

Isle of Wight

English   Channel

	United Kingdom
	Republic of Ireland

100 miles

100 km   200 km

15 *GREAT BRITAIN*

AVANT DE COMMENCER...

Great Britain is a grouping of **three countries**: England, Scotland and Wales. **United Kingdom** is a grouping of **four countries**: England, Scotland, Wales and Northern Ireland.

England is the largest of the three countries and the dominant power of the British Isles. The government of England is a **constitutional monarchy**, one of the rare western democracies that has kept a monarch. Real political power remains with the **Prime Minister**, though, and his or her ministers in the government.

The Queen and the Royal Family are largely figureheads, but their duties are mostly ceremonial. The Queen serves as a symbol of English pride and history, and the actions and statements of the Royal Family are closely watched by millions of Englishmen and others around the world.

Références

Films
If (Lindsay Anderson, 1968). *Gandhi* (Richard Attenborough, 1982).

VOCABULAIRE UTILE

figurehead: figure de proue
duty: devoir
pride: fierté
to defeat: vaincre
ruler: dirigeant
to lay the foundations: poser les fondations
to claim: revendiquer, réclamer
beheaded: décapité
the Pope: le Pape
playwright: auteur dramatique
rule: empire, autorité, domination

general election: élections législatives
to appoint: nommer
M.P.'s, Members of Parliament : députés
a bill: un projet de loi
policy: politique
to debate: débattre, discuter
peer: pair (du royaume)
to inherit: hériter
to bestow: conférer, accorder
the right wing: la droite (politique)
the left wing: la gauche (politique)

the Establishment: la société conformiste, « la bonne société »
to support: soutenir
free: gratuit
attended: fréquenté
public schools: écoles privées
college: université
to spread (spread, spread): s'étendre
a saying: un dicton
The sun sets...: Le soleil se couche...
first-class: de premier ordre

Important dates in English history

1066: England is defeated by the Normans at the battle of **Hastings. William of Normandy** is the new ruler, and for the next three centuries, the language of the Court will be French.

1215: The Anglo-Norman nobles force **King John** to sign **the Magna Carta**, which restrains the power of the King and lays the foundation for modern English democracy.

1337: The start of the **Hundred Years' War** between the rulers in France and those in England.

1453-1497: The War of the Roses. The Duke of York claims the throne of Henry VI, of the House of Lancaster.

1509-1547: The reign of Henry VIII, who had six wives, two of whom were beheaded. King Henry broke with the Pope in Rome and **established the Church of England in 1534**.

1558-1603: The reign of Queen Elizabeth. The **Elizabethan Period** is one of England's richest in terms of culture.

1564: The birth of **William Shakespeare**, perhaps the greatest playwright and poet in the English language.

1649: King Charles I is beheaded. England is declared a Commonwealth.

1653-1658: The rule of **Oliver Cromwell**, the English "dictator".

1776: The American colonies declare their independence from England.

1815: The British Army defeats Napoleon at **Waterloo.**

1837-1901: The rule of **Queen Victoria** and the consolidation of the British Empire.

1940-1941: The Battle of Britain. London and other cities are bombed by the Nazis.

The structure of the English government

The government is comprised of the **Prime Minister**, the **other Ministers** and the **Secretaries of State**.

The Prime Minister is the leader of the Party that wins the general election, held at least once every five years. The Queen officially appoints the Prime Minister.

The Prime Minister selects **the Ministers**, who must belong to either the House of Commons or the House of Lords. The most important Ministers form **the Cabinet**, which meets at the Prime Minister's residence **at 10 Downing Street**, near the Parliament.

The Parliament meets in the Palace of Westminster. It is comprised of **the House of Commons** and **the House of Lords**.

There are about **600 M.P.'s**, or Members of Parliament, in the House of Commons. Bills are introduced here, and the government's policy is debated.

The House of Lords is comprised of **Peers**, who are either hereditary peers (the title of Lord is inherited) or life peers (the title is bestowed by the Queen).

Political Parties

The two major parties in England are **the Conservative Party**, the party of the **right wing** Establishment, and the **Labour Party**, the party of the **left wing** that is traditionally supported by the middle and working classes.

English education system

There are two types of schools in England: **state schools**, which are free and are attended by the majority of English schoolchildren, and **public schools**, which are expensive and are attended by the children of the elite English families.

The public schools such as **Eton** and **Harrow** are known the world over, and many of England's most famous statesmen and business leaders have attended them.

Children under 5 years of age attend **Nursery School**. From the ages of 5 to 11, they attend **Primary School**, and from 11 to 17, **Comprehensive School**.

Students then take the exams for the **General Certificate of Secondary Education** (G.C.S.E.), and can go on to third education. Their placement in the best universities depends upon how well they do on their G.C.E. 'A' levels, and their performance in Comprehensive School.

In the universities, students study three or four years for their **Bachelor's Degree** (= *licence*). They can continue two more years for their **Master's Degree** (= *maîtrise*), and then another few years for the **Doctorate**, the **Ph.D** (= *thèse de 3ᵉ cycle*).

Today

At the beginning of the 20th century, the British Empire spread around the world, the richest and most powerful on earth. There was a saying: "The sun never sets on the British Empire." Since the end of World War II, however, England has lost nearly all of its colonial possessions, such as India and South Africa.

Today, England is no longer a first-class military or economic power. But British excellence is still found in other areas, such as its university system which is one of the world's best, with the famous **Oxford and Cambridge universities**, or in its televised media, which is of very high quality, generally.

In the arts, England remains strong, with dynamic activity in painting, literature, theatre, cinema and music.

16 IRELAND

AVANT DE COMMENCER...

Ireland is a country of ancient origins. There are elaborate folk legends that tell of **the heroes of the Celtic people who settled in Ireland about 500 B.C.** Even today, there is a deep, poetic beauty in much of the Irish countryside that seems timeless. Perhaps this is what has inspired so many of the great Irish poets, novelists and playwrights. For a tiny country of only **3.5 million people**, its literary output has been extraordinary.

It is impossible to speak of Ireland without speaking of England. **For centuries, the English dominated the Irish, who did not achieve partial political independence until 1921.** But even this agreement left **Northern Ireland,** or **Ulster, under British control**. This has been the cause of generations of fighting and bloodshed, which continues today.

Références

Films
The Field (Jim Sheridan, 1990). *The Commitments* (Alan Parker, 1991). *A Prayer for the Dying* (M. Hodges, 1987).

folk legend : légendes folkloriques ou populaires
to settle: s'installer
500 B.C. (500 before Christ): 500 avant Jésus-Christ
timeless: éternel
novelist: romancier
playwright: auteur dramatique
tiny: minuscule
output: production
to achieve: atteindre

agreement: accord
bloodshed: effusion de sang
to overrun (overran, overrun): se rendre maître de, occuper
to found: fonder
to defeat: vaincre
to invade: envahir
to crush: écraser
failure: perte (des récoltes)
crop: récolte
uprising: soulèvement
to fail: échouer

act: loi
bloody: sanglant
Easter Day: le jour de Pâques
to submit: se soumettre à
to support: soutenir
to strengthen: renforcer
outlawed: déclaré hors-la-loi
stifling: étouffant
struggle: lutte
European Economic Community : Marché commun
decade: décennie

143

Important dates in Irish history

795: **The Vikings** overrun Ireland. They found several cities, including Dublin, the capital. They are finally defeated by Gaelic forces in the 11th century.

1169: **The Normans and Anglos invade Ireland.**

1541: Henry VIII of England is declared King of Ireland. He tries to impose the rule of the Church of England on the Catholic Irish. Here begins the long domination by the English.

1649: Cromwell crushes the Irish armed resistance that has risen against the English occupying forces.

1845-1849: **The Potato Famine**, caused by the failure of the potato crop, causes hundreds of thousands of Irish to emigrate to the United States.

1848: The leaders of **Young Ireland**, a nationalist group, try to cause an uprising of the people, but fail.

1914: After decades of efforts, the English parliament finally votes a **Home Rule Act**, by which Ireland will be able to govern itself, with less interference from England.

1916: **Bloody Sunday.** On Easter Day, Irish Republican supporters are shot by the British army.

1921: The English give the status of **dominion** to Ireland, meaning the country must still submit to the British King.

1937: The constitution of the Republic of Ireland is passed, and Southern Ireland becomes an independent country, the Eire, but Ulster remains attached to the British crown.

Since the late 1960's, the violence in Northern Ireland has dominated the world news about Ireland. **The Catholic minority in Ulster**, supported by the Catholic Irish Republic in the South, but oppressed in the North, has tried to strengthen its political and economic position. But **the Protestant majority** has refused to give up its privileges.

Violence on both sides, most spectacularly by the outlawed Irish Republican Army (I.R.A.), has been devastating. The British Army still occupies Ulster, and no quick solution to this problem is in sight.

Irish Literature

Samuel Beckett, James Joyce, George Bernard Shaw, William Butler Yeats and **Sean O'Casey** are only a few of the world famous Irish writers of the 20th century. The impact of Ireland on world literature has been great. But many of Ireland's best writers found the strict Catholic mentality of the country stifling, and they preferred to live and write abroad.

Today

Irish history is full of tragedy of the **long struggle for independence from England.** Ireland has also struggled with itself, against domination by the Catholic church that has sometimes alienated its most creative people. But Ireland is becoming a more active member of the European Economic Community, less dependent on England, and more a part of modern Europe.

Notes

■■■■■ *Testez vos connaissances en civilisation avec ce questionnaire à choix multiples.*

Entourez la réponse correcte.

Vous avez un doute ?
Consultez les pages...

1/ **What document serves as the basis for American law and government?**
a) The Declaration of Independence.
b) The War Powers Act.
c) The United States Constitution.

85-88 ———

2/ **When was the U.S. Constitution adopted by the States?**
a) 1776.
b) 1788.
c) 1808.

85-88 ———

3/ **What was the main reason why American colonies fought the War for Independence?**
a) They wanted less tax on tea.
b) They hated the British.
c) They wanted to gain their economic and political freedom.

85-88 ———

4/ **How many colonies were there originally when the United States was founded?**
a) Thirteen.
b) Six.
c) Fifty.

85-88 ———

5/ **What was the principal cause of the American Civil War?**
a) The assassination of President Lincoln.
b) General Sherman's March to the Sea.
c) Slavery.

89-91 ———

6/ **Who were the Abolitionists?**
a) The Party of President Jefferson Davis.
b) The Northern anti-slavery Party.
c) The Southern plantation owners.

89-91 ———

7/ **What was the Emancipation Proclamation?**
a) A part of the Constitution.
b) A law proposed by the Southern slave owners.
c) Lincoln's act to abolish slavery.

89-91 ———

8/ The Great Depression was started by what event?   93-94 ———
a) World War II.
b) The election of Herbert Hoover as President.
c) The Stock Market crash of 1929.

9/ The Great Depression ended with what event?   93-94 ———
a) Prohibition.
b) American industry's preparation for World War II.
c) The election of Franklin D. Roosevelt as President.

10/ The New Deal was: 93-94 ———
a) a plan to prepare American industry for World War II.
b) a plan to fight the « bootleggers ».
c) Roosevelt's plan of government assistance to people in poverty.

11/ How many times was Franklin Roosevelt elected President of the United States?   93-94 ———
a) Four.
b) Three.
c) Two.

12/ Who won the Korean War?   95-97 ———
a) America.
b) North Korea and China.
c) No one. It ended in a stalemate.

13/ What does the McCarthy era symbolize today?   95-97 ———
a) The triumph of democracy.
b) Anti-communism, racism, anti-semitism.
c) The failure of communism.

14/ Where does the term "witch hunt" come from?   95-97 ———
a) From the Puritan era in America.
b) From popular science fiction.
c) From communist propaganda.

15/ What is the system of checks and balances?   99-101 ———
a) A scientific system of measurement.
b) The system, created in the Constitution, that guarantees a balance of power in government.
c) The way of determining the correct number of Representatives for each State.

147

16/ How many Representatives are there in the House?   99-101 ——
   a) 435.
   b) 50.
   c) 100.

17/ How many Senators are there in the Senate?   99-101 ——
   a) 435.
   b) 50.
   c) 100.

18/ How many waves of immigration have there been in   103-105 ——
American history?
   a) Six.
   b) Three.
   c) Two.

19/ The Third Wave of immigrants occurred in what   103-105 ——
decades?
   a) 1970's and 1980's.
   b) 1920's and 1930's.
   c) 1880's and 1890's.

20/ The Third Wave was made up of what two groups of   103-105 ——
people?
   a) Italians and Scandinavians.
   b) Russians and Poles.
   c) Hispanics and Asians.

21/ How is the idea of "The Melting Pot" seen today?   103-105 ——
   a) It is considered admirable and important by everyone.
   b) It is considered an old idea that no longer reflects reality
   today.
   c) It is considered a shameful mistake.

22/ When were the first slaves brought to America?   107-109 ——
   a) At the start of the Civil War, in 1865.
   b) In 1808.
   c) In 1619, a year before the Puritans arrived.

23/ Blacks make up what percentage of America's popu-   107-109 ——
lation?
   a) About one-tenth.
   b) About one-third.
   c) About one-fifth.

24/ When was the Civil Rights Act passed?　　107-109 ——
a) 1865.
b) 1808.
c) 1964.

25/ Who was Martin Luther King?　　107-109 ——
a) American President in the 1960's.
b) The most famous black leader of the twentieth century.
c) A black slave during the Civil War.

26/ When was the Vietnam War fought?　　111-113 ——
a) 1968-1972.
b) 1975-1980.
c) 1965-1975.

27/ How many Americans were killed in Vietnam?　　111-113 ——
a) 150,000.
b) 55,000.
c) Hundreds of thousands.

28/ How many Vietnamese were killed in Vietnam from　111-113 ——
1965 to 1975?
a) 55,000.
b) 150,000.
c) Hundreds of thousands.

29/ Why couldn't the American military defeat the Viet　111-113 ——
Cong?
a) The Viet Cong were skilled at guerilla warfare, and had more will to win.
b) The Americans had too much technology.
c) The Americans didn't have enough soldiers.

30/ The largest religious group today in the United　　115-117 ——
States is:
a) Catholics.
b) Protestants.

31/ What does the U.S. Constitution say about the rela-　115-117 ——
tionship between church and state?
a) Church and state must always remain separate.
b) The church should play an active role in government.
c) The government should enforce its laws on the church.

32/ How many Americans say they belong to a specific 115-117 religion?
a) One-half.
b) One-third.
c) Two-thirds.

33/ The most respected newspaper in the U.S. is: 119-121
a) the *Washington Post.*
b) the *New York Times.*
c) NBC.

34/ How many Americans get the news through television? 119-121
a) One-half.
b) One-third.
c) Two-thirds.

35/ Critics complain that television network news shows 119-121 are:
a) too superficial.
b) too long.
c) too intellectual.

36/ Why are there so many guns in America today? 123-125
a) The U.S. Constitution guarantees the right to own guns.
b) Americans fear an invasion by the Russians.
c) Americans traditionally like to collect antique firearms.

37/ How many Americans were victims of violent crime 123-125 in 1989?
a) 5 million.
b) 37 million.
c) 110 million.

38/ What American city has the worst violent crime 123-125 problem today?
a) Los Angeles.
b) New York.
c) Washington.

39/ How many Americans lived below the poverty line in 123-125 1990?
a) 10 to 20 million.
b) more than 30 million.
c) 60 to 70 million.

40/ **How many people live in New York today?** 127-129 ——
   a) 3 million.
   b) 5 million.
   c) 9 million.

41/ **Los Angeles has more per capita than any other** 127-129 ——
American city:
   a) personal income.
   b) immigrant workers.
   c) automobiles.

42/ **The Puritan ideal of a close family:** 131-134 ——
   a) is still present everywhere.
   b) ended with the Puritans.
   c) no longer exists for many Americans today.

43/ **The ideal of a "campus" at American colleges means:** 131-134 ——
   a) that colleges are very expensive.
   b) that there is an entire social life at college.
   c) that colleges are difficult to enter.

44/ **State colleges in America are:** 131-134 ——
   a) less expensive than private colleges.
   b) more expensive than private colleges.
   c) harder to enter than private colleges.

45/ **The American work ethic means:** 131-134 ——
   a) that you will become a "workaholic".
   b) that it is socially acceptable to be unemployed.
   c) that hard work is the honest way to advance.

46/ **Where did jazz originate?** 135-137 ——
   a) In New York's Harlem district.
   b) In Chicago.
   c) In the southern city of New Orleans.

47/ **The first jazz musicians were:** 135-137 ——
   a) slaves or descendants of slaves.
   b) Blacks looking for jobs in Chicago.
   c) victims of the Great Depression.

48/ **When was the first "talkie" made?** 135-137 ——
   a) In the late 19th century.
   b) In 1940.
   c) In 1927.

49/ When did Hollywood's Golden era end?   135-137 ——
a) In the 1920's.
b) In the late 1940's, with the invention of television.
c) In the 1930's, with the Great Depression.

50/ What is United Kingdom a grouping of?   139-142 ——
a) England, Scotland and Wales.
b) England, Scotland, Wales and Northern Ireland.

51/ Who possesses the real political power   139-142 ——
in England today?
a) The Queen.
b) The House of Lords.
c) The Prime Minister.

52/ English government today is: 139-142 ——
a) a monarchy.
b) a constitutional monarchy.
c) a presidential democracy.

53/ The House of Commons meets in: 139-142 ——
a) Westminster.
b) 10 Downing St.
c) The House of Lords.

54/ What is a public school in England?   139-142 ——
a) a private school.
b) a state school.

55/ In 1847, the main reason why many Irish   143-145 ——
emigrated to the United States was:
a) religious persecution.
b) promise of jobs in New York.
c) the Potato Famine in Ireland.

56/ Ulster or Northern Ireland has: 143-145 ——
a) a Catholic majority.
b) a Protestant majority.

Les jokers

- **PETIT DICTIONNAIRE DES PERSONNALITÉS**
- **LES MOTS CLÉS DE LA CIVILISATION ANGLO-SAXONNE**
- **BRITISH AND AMERICAN ENGLISH**
- **VERBES IRRÉGULIERS**

PETIT DICTIONNAIRE
DES PERSONNALITÉS

Vous les avez rencontrées. Rappelez-vous qui elles sont.

Nous avons imprimé en rouge le nom des personnalités littéraires.

Allen, Woody (1935-   )
Born Allen Stewart Koenigsberg. Contemporary American playwright, filmmaker, author, and actor. Famous for his typical New York jewish humour and his sense of the comic and social commentary. His films include *Annie Hall* (1977), *Manhattan* (1977), *Zelig* (1983), *Purple Rose of Cairo* (1985), *Hannah and Her Sisters* (1986), *Radio Days* (1987).

Armstrong, Louis (1900-1971)
Also known as "Satchmo". One of the best known American jazz musicians; a trumpet player, singer, band leader, and song writer. One of the first and best in the genres of swing music and "scat" singing.

Baldwin, James (1924-1987)
He grew up in Harlem (New-York). He left for France in 1948. Essayist, playwright and novelist, he was a spokesman for Blacks and the civil rights movements. He wrote: *Notes of a Native Son* (1955), *Nobody Knows my Name* (1961), *Go Tell It on the Mountain* (1953).

Beckett, Samuel (1906-1989)
Irish writer who settled in France from 1938 to his death. He was one of the major figures of the "theatre of the Absurd". He wrote novels (*Molloy*, 1951) and plays (*En attendant Godot*, 1953), mostly in French. He was awarded the Nobel Prize for Literature in 1969.

Beecher Stowe, Harriet (1811-1896)
A 19th century American novelist. Her book *Uncle Tom's Cabin* published in 1852, was used by Abolitionists to make people conscious of the condition of slaves in the U.S. The book has been translated into over thirty languages.

Brink, André (1935-   )
A South African author and lecturer at Rhodes University. His works include: *Looking On Darkness, A Dry White Season* (1979) and *The Wall of the Plague* (1984).

Buchwald, Art (1925-   )
A columnist for the *New York Times* and the *Washington Post*. His column appears in the *International Herald Tribune* which uses both of these newspapers as sources.

Chaplin, Charlie (1889-1977)
Comic English actor and film director, beginning with silent films and

continuing after the advent of sound movies. He left the U.S. during the McCarthy era because he was a victim of the "witch hunt". Some great films include: *City Lights* (1931), *Modern Times* (1936), and *The Great Dictator* (1940). He is most famous as the character "the little tramp".

Churchill, Sir Winston (1874-1965)

English politician. The Prime Minister of Great Britain from 1940 to 1945 and again from 1951 to 1955. He played a very important role during World War II as one of the principal leaders of the Allied forces.

Davis, Angela (1944-   )

A black American civil rights activist. During the '70s she was arrested on a false charge of murder and conspiracy, for which she was acquitted. She continues to be involved in politics. She was twice the vice-president candidate for the U.S. communist party.

Davis, Miles (1926-1991)

Black American jazz trumpet player. First a "bop" musician in New York. Known as a modern jazz musician, he is especially noted for his own style of improvisation.

Dickens, Charles (1812-1870)

A Victorian era British author of novels and short stories. His well known characters include Ebenezer Scrooge, Oliver Twist, and Samuel Pickwick. Some works: *Oliver Twist* (1838), *David Copperfield* (1849), *Little Dorrit* (1855).

Disney, Walt (1901-1966)

American animated film maker. Two of his most famous characters are Mickey Mouse and Donald Duck. He made many animated adaptations of fairy tales including *Snow White and the Seven Dwarfs* and *Cinderella*. The Walt Disney Corp. still produces films today.

Dos Passos, John (1896-1970)

American journalist and author. Was a war correspondent during World War II before becoming a full-time writer. Some works: *Manhattan Transfer* (1925), *U.S.A.: The 42nd Parallel* (1930), *Big Money* (1936).

Dylan, Bob (1941-   )

American folk and pop singer. He was one of the main figures of the underground American youth in the 60's. *Blowing in the Wind* (1962) is one of his most famous songs.

Eisenhower, Dwight (1890-1969)

34th President of the U.S.A. Served two consecutive terms starting in '52 and '56. During World War II he was the commander in chief of the Allied Forces in Europe. In 1950, commander in chief of NATO.

Faulkner, William (1897-1962)

An American novelist. *The Sound and the Fury* (1929) is one of his most well known works. In 1949, he won the Nobel Prize for Literature.

Fitzgerald, Ella (1918-   )

Black American jazz and blues singer. She is especially known for her "scat" singing improvisation, the most famous example of which is found in the song *A Tisket A Tasket*.

Fitzgerald, F. Scott (1896-1940)
American author of short stories and novels. One of his most famous novels is *The Great Gatsby* (1925). He was one of the American expatriate community living in Paris during the 20s. This group is also known as the "lost generation".

Gandhi, Mohandas Karamchand (1869-1948)
Known as the "Mahatma", meaning "the wise man". Studied law in London and practised law until 1893. He was President of the Indian National Congress in 1925. Although Hindu himself, he preached Hindu-Moslem unity. He was an advocate for nonviolence in India's struggle for independence from Great Britain, and for pacifism in all circumstances. He was assassinated by a Hindu in 1948.

Haley, Alex (1921-   )
A black American writer. His most famous book is *Roots* (1976). This book chronicles the history of Haley's own family from Africa through slavery to contemporary American life. It was the result of twelve years of research.

Hemingway, Ernest (1899-1961)
An American writer. He, like Fitzgerald, was one of the "lost generation" living in Paris between the wars. He began writing as a newspaper reporter. In 1954 he won the Nobel Prize for Literature. His best known books are *A Farewell to Arms* (1929) and *For Whom the Bell Tolls* (1940).

Hitchcock, Alfred (1899-1980)
Born in Britain, he became a film director in Hollywood. He was the master of the suspense film. Among his many films are *The Thirty-Nine Steps* (1935), *North by Northwest* (*La Mort aux Trousses*, 1959) and *The Birds* (1963).

Huxley, Aldous (1894-1963)
A British author best known for his novel, *Brave New World* (1932). This book details life in a disturbing futuristic society.

Jefferson, Thomas (1743-1826)
American politician. Part of the beginning of the movement for independence from Britain. He was Secretary of State under President Washington and was the 3rd President of the U.S.A. Serving terms beginning in 1801 and 1805. He was for less federal power and more rights to the States. Extremely pro democracy.

Jong, Erica (1942-   )
A contemporary American author whose novels address feminist issues. Two of her best known works are *Fear of Flying* and *Fanny*.

Joyce, James (1882-1941)
Irish writer who lived in Trieste (Italy), Switzerland and France (Paris). His most famous novel, *Ulysses* (1922), revolutionized the European literature of his time.

Kazan, Elia (1909-   )
Born in Constantinople, he became an actor and then a filmmaker in the U.S.A. First a member of the Group Theatre and then in 1948, formed the Actor's Studio with Lee Strass-

157

berg. He was known as having leftist political ideas but during the trials under McCarthy he was a witness against Arthur Miller. Well-known films include *A Streetcar Named Desire* (1951), *East of Eden* (1955) and *America, America* (1963).

Kennedy, John Fitzgerald (1917-1963)

35th President of the U.S.A. In 1960 he became the first Catholic and youngest man elected to that office. He began U.S. involvement in Vietnam. He forced the U.S.S.R. to withdraw their missiles from Cuba during the "Cuban Missile Crisis". He wrote *Profiles in Courage,* for which he won a Pulitzer Prize. He was assassinated in 1963.

King, Martin Luther, Jr., (1929-1968)

A leader of the black civil rights movement in the U.S.A. during the '60s. He was a black Baptist minister and was a nonviolence advocate in the struggle for racial equality. He received the Nobel Peace Prize in 1964. He was assassinated in 1968.

Lawrence, David Herbert (1885-1930)

An early 20th century British author. He is known for his open treatment of sex and his radical ideas concerning the society of his time. His works include *Sons and Lovers, Women in Love, Lady Chatterley's Lover* (1928) which was initially banned in the U.S. and in England.

Lincoln, Abraham (1809-1865)

American politician. He began his career as a lawyer in Illinois. In 1860 he was elected the 16th President of the U.S.A. He was a Republican and known to be anti-slavery. With his election the South seceded from the Union. During the Civil War, his main goal was to preserve the Union. In 1863 he declared all slaves in America free. In 1865 he was assassinated.

Mitchell, Margaret (1900-1949)

An American novelist. She researched for ten years before publishing her most famous book, *Gone With the Wind* (1936), a novel about the Civil War and Reconstruction, based in Georgia.

Nixon, Richard (1913-   )

37th President of the U.S.A. He was elected for two consecutive terms beginning in 1968 and 1972. He was forced to resign in 1973 during the "Watergate Scandal".

O'Ceasey, Sean (1880-1964)

Irish dramatist, his political and patriotic convictions led him to set the Irish people as the protagonist of his plays (*The Plough and the Stars,* 1926).

Orwell, George (1903-1950)

An early 20th century English author, born Eric Blair. His best known works are *Animal Farm* and *1984,* a novel depicting a totalitarian futuristic society dominated by the ever watchful "Big Brother".

Poe, Edgar Allan (1809-1849)

American poet and author of short horror stories. Well-known works include *"The Fall of the House of Usher"*, *"The Cask of Amontillado"*, and the poems *"The Bells"* and *"The Raven"*.

Roosevelt, Franklin D. (1882-1945)
32nd President of the U.S.A. Elected for four consecutive terms beginning in 1932, 1936, 1940 and 1944. He initiated the "New Deal" during the depression.

Roth, Phillip (1933-   )
American novelist. His collection of short fiction, *Goodbye Columbus*, won the National Book Award in 1960. Other works include *Letting Go* (1961) and *Portnoy's Complaint* (1969).

Shakespeare, William (1564-1616)
He is known as one of the greatest poets and playwrights of the English language. He began his work in theatre as an actor, but assumed the roles of director and writer as well. His plays can be divided into history plays, such as *Richard III*, comedies, such as *A Midsummer's Night's Dream*, and tragedies, such as *Hamlet* and *Romeo and Juliet*.

Shaw, George Bernard (1856-1950)
Irish writer, he was mostly a playwright. In his plays, he criticized the prejudices and conventional morality of the Victorian era (*Pygmalion*, 1913). He won the Nobel Prize for Literature in 1925.

Steinbeck, John (1902-1968)
An American author who often dealt with the subjects of the Great Depression and the outsider. In 1962 he was awarded the Nobel Prize for Literature. Three of this best known works are: *Of Mice and Men* (1937), *The Grapes of Wrath* (1939), and *East of Eden* (1952).

Stuyvesant, Peter (1592-1672)
Dutch founder of New Amsterdam which later became New York. Surrendered to the British in 1664.

Taylor, Frederick (1856-1915)
American engineer and businessman. Founder of the efficient production method known as taylorism, a method of producing the most actions in the least amount of time.

Thatcher, Margaret (1925-   )
Known as the "Iron Lady". Elected British Prime Minister in 1979, defeating the Labour Party. She resigned in 1990.

Twain, Mark (1835-1910)
"Nom de plume" of the 19th century American author, Samuel Clemmons. His stories most often occur in the South along the Mississippi River. His works include *The Adventures of Tom Sawyer* (1876) and *The Adventures of Huckleberry Finn* (1885), the title characters of which have come to represent "America".

Washington, George (1732-1799)
American general during the American Revolution. Became the first President of the U.S.A. in 1789. Washington D.C., the federal capital, is named after him.

Whitman, Walt (1819-1892)
A 19th century American poet. He began his writing career as a journalist and editor of a daily newspaper. His poems are gathered in ten different collections, all bearing the title *Leaves of Grass*. The first edition contained ten poems, the last 369.

Woolf, Virginia (1882-1941)

British author of novels, short stories, essays and a play. She was a member of "the Bloomsbury Circle" literary group. Known for having insanity spells throughout her life, she committed suicide in 1941. Her works include *Mrs. Dalloway* (1925), *Orlando* (1928), *A Room of one's Own* (1929), and *The Death of the Moth* (1942), published after her death.

Wright, Richard (1908-1960)

He lived in Chicago. He was influenced by marxism but, disappointed with the Communist Party and the U.S.A., he left the U.S.A. for France in 1947. He is one of the major figures of the black American literature. He wrote: *Native Son* (1940), *Black Boy* (1945), *The Outsider* (1953).

Yeats, William Butler (1865-1939)

Irish poet and dramatist. His inspiration was deeply rooted in the Irish tradition (*Deidr*, 1907). He was a leader of the Irish cultural revival and was awarded the Nobel Prize for Literature in 1923.

LES MOTS CLÉS DE LA
CIVILISATION ANGLO-SAXONNE

Vous les connaissez. Retenez leur sens exact.

Bootlegger
A person who made and sold illegal alcohol during the Prohibition era in America (1920-1933).

New Deal
President Franklin Roosevelt's program of government assistance to people in poverty during the "Great Depression" in the 1930's.

Moral Majority
A powerful religious group of fundamentalists, led by Reverend Jerry Falwell, who is influent in national politics, fighting for the return to the most conservative values in America.

Prohibition
The period from 1920 to 1933 when the American Congress made it illegal to manufacture or sell alcohol in the United States.

Abolitionist
An anti-slavery person, someone who was in favour of the abolition of slavery during the years of the American Civil War.

Ku Klux Klan
A secret society of people who believe in white supremacy. They have been known to intimidate and even murder Blacks, Jews and foreigners.

Civil Rights
Refers to the act of Congress in 1964 that guaranteed equal treatment to Blacks and other minorities in America.

NATO
North Atlantic Treaty Organization, the group of western nations who joined military forces as a defense against attack from the Soviet Union or its allies after World War II.

Sit-in
A form of protest, popular in the 1960's, in which the protestors illegally but peacefully occupy a building or other area until forced out by the police.

Checks and balances
The system, devised by the U.S. Constitution, that allows for each of the three branches of government to balance the power of the other two, and act as a check against abuse of power.

Confederates
The Southern States that seceded from the United States during the American Civil War, the pro-slavery States.

Melting Pot
The term referring to America in the 19th and early 20th centuries, and the social pressure on new immigrants to conform to American lifestyle.

The American Dream
Generally refers to the desire to become prosperous through hard work, to overcome hardship and achieve success in life.

U.S. Marines
The branch of the U.S. military considered the toughest. The Marines are traditionally the first soldiers into battle in the event of war.

The Commonwealth
Association of former colonies which were part of the British Empire. They recognize the British Sovereign as their honorary chief.

Dominion
Refers to any of the countries, such as Canada or Australia, that were once members of the British Commonwealth of Nations.

I.R.A.
The Irish Republican Army, a secret organization formed to fight for independence from Great Britain. Its goal today is unification of Northern Ireland with the Republic of Ireland in the South.

BRITISH
AND AMERICAN ENGLISH

"England and America are two countries separated by the same language."

(George Bernard SHAW)

British	American	French
aerial	antenna	*antenne (radio-télé)*
anywhere	anyplace	*quelque part*
autumn	fall	*automne*
banknote	bill	*billet de banque*
bank holiday	national holiday	*jour férié*
bill	check	*addition, facture*
bonnet	hood	*capot*
boot	trunk	*coffre (d'automobile)*
braces	suspenders	*bretelles*
caretaker, porter	janitor	*concierge, gardien*
car	automobile	*voiture*
centre	center	*centre*
chemist's	drugstore	*pharmacie*
chips	French fries	*frites*
Christian name	first name	*prénom*
cinema	movie house, movie theater	*(salle de) cinéma*
city centre	downtown	*centre ville*
class	grade	*classe*
colour	color	*couleur*
condom	rubber	*préservatif*
crisps	chips	*chips*
crossroads	intersection	*carrefour*
cupboard	closet	*placard*
dinner-jacket	tuxedo	*smoking, tenue de soirée*
Don't mention it!	You're welcome!	*Il n'y a pas de quoi !*
ex-serviceman	veteran	*ancien combattant*

163

British	American	French
film	movie	*film*
flat	apartment	*appartement*
fortnight	two weeks	*deux semaines,*
		une quinzaine
full stop	period	*point*
grammar school	high school	*collège*
ground floor	first floor	*rez-de-chaussée*
(first floor)	(second floor...)	*(1er étage)*
handbag	purse, pocket-book	*sac à main*
holiday	vacation	*vacances*
hoover (to)	vacuum (to)	*passer l'aspirateur*
ill	sick	*malade*
interval	intermission	*entracte*
letter-box, pillar-box	mail box	*boîte aux lettres*
lift	elevator	*ascenseur*
lorry	truck	*camion*
luggage	baggage	*bagages*
mark	grade	*note*
motorway	freeway	*autoroute*
pavement	sidewalk	*trottoir*
pedestrian (zebra) crossing	crosswalk	*passage piétons*
petrol	gas, gasoline	*essence*
postal code	zip code	*code postal*
prison	jail	*prison*
programme	program	*programme*
public school	private school	*école privée*
queue	line	*queue*
return ticket	round trip ticket	*billet aller-retour*
rubbish	garbage, trash	*ordures*
second hand	used	*d'occasion, usagé*
single ticket	one way ticket	*billet aller simple*

British	American	French
spirits	liquor	*alcool*
stand for (to)	run for (to)	*être candidat à*
state school	public school	*école publique*
student, schoolboy	student	*étudiant, écolier*
– 1st year undergraduate	– freshman	*– étudiant de 1ʳᵉ année*
– 2nd year undergraduate	– sophomore	*– étudiant de 2ᵉ année*
– 3rd year student	– junior	*– étudiant de 3ᵉ année*
– 4th year student	– senior	*– étudiant de 4ᵉ année*
surname	last name	*nom de famille*
sweets	candies	*bonbons*
tap	faucet	*robinet*
taxi	cab	*taxi*
telephone booth (box)	payphone	*cabine téléphonique*
theatre	theater	*théâtre*
timetable	schedule	*horaire*
tin	can	*boîte de conserve*
trousers	pants	*pantalon*
tyre	tire	*pneu*
underground, tube	subway	*métro*

VERBES IRRÉGULIERS

a
awake [ə/ei]	awoke [ə/əu]	awoken [ə/əu]	*se réveiller*

b
be [i:]	was [ɔ]/were [ə:]	been [i:]	*être*
bear [eə]	bore [ɔə]	borne [ɔ:]	*supporter*
beat [i:]	beat [i:]	beaten [i:]	*battre*
become [ʌ]	became [ei]	become [ʌ]	*devenir*
begin [i]	began [æ]	begun [ʌ]	*commencer*
bend [e]	bent [e]	bent [e]	*courber, se pencher*
bet [e]	bet [e]	bet [e]	*parier*
bite [ai]	bit [i]	bitten [i]	*mordre*
blow [əu]	blew [u:]	blown [əu]	*souffler*
break [ei]	broke [əu]	broken [əu]	*briser*
breed [i:]	bred [e]	bred [e]	*élever (enfants, bétail)*
bring [i]	brought [ɔ:]	brought [ɔ:]	*apporter*
build [i]	built [i]	built [i]	*bâtir*
burn [ə:]	burnt [ə:]	burnt [ə:]	*brûler*
burst [ə:]	burst [ə:]	burst [ə:]	*éclater*
buy [ai]	bought [ɔ:]	bought [ɔ:]	*acheter*

c
cast [ɑ:]	cast [ɑ:]	cast [ɑ:]	*jeter*
catch [æ]	caught [ɔ:]	caught [ɔ:]	*attraper*
choose [u:]	chose [əu]	chosen [əu]	*choisir*
come [ʌ]	came [ei]	come [ʌ]	*venir*
cost [ɔ]	cost [ɔ]	cost [ɔ]	*coûter*
creep [i:]	crept [e]	crept [e]	*ramper*
cut [ʌ]	cut [ʌ]	cut [ʌ]	*couper*

d
deal [i:]	dealt [e]	dealt [e]	*distribuer, traiter*
dig [i]	dug [ʌ]	dug [ʌ]	*creuser*
do [u:]	did [i]	done [ʌ]	*faire*
draw [ɔ:]	drew [u:]	drawn [ɔ:]	*dessiner*
dream [i:]	dreamt [e]	dreamt [e]	*rêver*

drink [i]	drank [æ]	drunk [ʌ]	*boire*
drive [ai]	drove [əu]	driven [i]	*conduire*

e _____

eat [i:]	ate [e]	eaten [i:]	*manger*

f _____

fall [ɔ:]	fell [e]	fallen [ɔ:]	*tomber*
feed [i:]	fed [e]	fed [e]	*nourrir*
feel [i:]	felt [e]	felt [e]	*(se) sentir, éprouver*
fight [ai]	fought [ɔ:]	fought [ɔ:]	*combattre*
find [ai]	found [au]	found [au]	*trouver*
fly [ai]	flew [u:]	flown [əu]	*voler, aller en avion*
forbid [ə/i]	forbade [ə/æ]	forbidden [ə/i]	*interdire*
foresee [ɔ:/i:]	foresaw [ɔ:/ɔ:]	foreseen [ɔ:/i:]	*prévoir*
forget [ə/e]	forgot [ə/ɔ]	forgotten [ə/ɔ]	*oublier*
forgive [ə/i]	forgave [ə/ei]	forgiven [ə/i]	*pardonner*
freeze [i:]	froze [əu]	frozen [əu]	*geler*

g _____

get [e]	got [ɔ]	got [ɔ]	*obtenir, devenir*
give [i]	gave [ei]	given [i]	*donner*
go [əu]	went [e]	gone [ɔ]	*aller*
grow [əu]	grew [u:]	grown [əu]	*grandir, faire pousser*

h _____

hang [æ]	hung [ʌ]	hung [ʌ]	*pendre, accrocher*
have [æ]	had [æ]	had [æ]	*avoir*
hear [iə]	heard [ə:]	heard [ə:]	*entendre*
hide [ai]	hid [i]	hidden [i]	*(se) cacher*
hit [i]	hit [i]	hit [i]	*frapper, atteindre*
hold [əu]	held [e]	held [e]	*tenir*
hurt [ə:]	hurt [ə:]	hurt [ə:]	*blesser, faire mal*

k _____

keep [i:]	kept [e]	kept [e]	*garder*
know [nəu]	knew [nju:]	known [nəun]	*savoir, connaître*

l _____

lay [ei]	laid [ei]	laid [ei]	*poser à plat*
lead [i:]	led [e]	led [e]	*mener*
lean [i:]	leant [e]	leant [e]	*s'appuyer*
leap [i:]	leapt [e]	leapt [e]	*sauter*
learn [ə:]	learnt [ə:]	learnt [ə:]	*apprendre*

168

leave [i:]	left [e]	left [e]	*laisser, quitter, partir*
lend [e]	lent [e]	lent [e]	*prêter*
let [e]	let [e]	let [e]	*laisser, permettre*
lie [ai]	lay [ei]	lain [ei]	*être étendu*
light [ai]	lit [i]	lit [i]	*allumer, éclairer*
lose [u:]	lost [ɔ]	lost [ɔ]	*perdre*

m

make [ei]	made [ei]	made [ei]	*faire, fabriquer*
mean [i:]	meant [e]	meant [e]	*signifier, vouloir dire*
meet [i:]	met [e]	met [e]	*(se) rencontrer*

o

overcome [əu/ə/ʌ]	overcame [əu/ə/ei]	overcome [əu/ə/ʌ]	*surmonter, vaincre*

p

pay [ei]	paid [ei]	paid [ei]	*payer*
put [u]	put [u]	put [u]	*mettre*

r

read [i:]	read [e]	read [e]	*lire*
ride [ai]	rode [əu]	ridden [i]	*aller (à cheval, à bicyclette)*
ring [i]	rang [æ]	rung [ʌ]	*sonner*
rise [ai]	rose [əu]	risen [i]	*s'élever*
run [ʌ]	ran [æ]	run [ʌ]	*courir*

s

say [ei]	said [e]	said [e]	*dire*
see [i:]	saw [ɔ:]	seen [i:]	*voir*
seek [i:]	sought [ɔ:]	sought [ɔ:]	*chercher*
sell [e]	sold [əu]	sold [əu]	*vendre*
send [e]	sent [e]	sent [e]	*envoyer*
set [e]	set [e]	set [e]	*fixer*
shake [ei]	shook [u]	shaken [ei]	*secouer*
shine [ai]	shone [ɔ]	shone [ɔ]	*briller*
shoot [u:]	shot [ɔ]	shot [ɔ]	*tirer, fusiller*
show [əu]	showed [əu]	shown [əu]	*montrer*
shut [ʌ]	shut [ʌ]	shut [ʌ]	*fermer*
sing [i]	sang [æ]	sung [ʌ]	*chanter*
sink [i]	sank [æ]	sunk [ʌ]	*sombrer, couler*
sit [i]	sat [æ]	sat [æ]	*être assis*

169

sleep [iː]	slept [e]	slept [e]	*dormir*
smell [e]	smelt [e]	smelt [e]	*sentir (odorat)*
speak [iː]	spoke [əu]	spoken [əu]	*parler*
spell [e]	spelt [e]	spelt [e]	*épeler*
spend [e]	spent [e]	spent [e]	*dépenser, passer (temps)*
spread [e]	spread [e]	spread [e]	*étaler, étendre*
spring [i]	sprang [æ]	sprung [ʌ]	*jaillir, bondir*
stand [æ]	stood [u]	stood [u]	*être debout*
steal [iː]	stole [əu]	stolen [əu]	*voler, dérober*
stick [i]	stuck [ʌ]	stuck [ʌ]	*coller*
strike [ai]	struck [ʌ]	struck [ʌ]	*frapper*
swear [eə]	swore [ɔə]	sworn [ɔː]	*jurer*
sweep [iː]	swept [e]	swept [e]	*balayer*
swim [i]	swam [æ]	swum [ʌ]	*nager*
swing [i]	swung [ʌ]	swung [ʌ]	*(se) balancer*

t

take [ei]	took [u]	taken [ei]	*prendre*
teach [iː]	taught [ɔː]	taught [ɔː]	*enseigner*
tear [eə]	tore [ɔə]	torn [ɔː]	*déchirer*
tell [e]	told [əu]	told [əu]	*dire, raconter*
think [i]	thought [ɔː]	thought [ɔː]	*penser*
throw [əu]	threw [uː]	thrown [əu]	*jeter, lancer*

u

undergo [ʌ/ə/əu]	underwent [ʌ/ə/e]	undergone [ʌ/ə/ɔ]	*subir*
understand [ʌ/ə/æ]	understood [ʌ/ə/u]	understood [ʌ/ə/u]	*comprendre*
undo [ʌ/uː]	undid [ʌ/i]	undone [ʌ/ʌ]	*défaire*
upset [ʌ/e]	upset [ʌ/e]	upset [ʌ/e]	*renverser, bouleverser*

w

wake (up) [ei]	woke [əu]	woken [əu]	*(se) réveiller*
wear [eə]	wore [ɔə]	worn [ɔː]	*porter (vêtements)*
weep [iː]	wept [e]	wept [e]	*pleurer*
win [i]	won [ʌ]	won [ʌ]	*gagner*
write [ai]	wrote [əu]	written [i]	*écrire*

L'épreuve du bac

- L'ÉPREUVE ÉCRITE
- L'ÉPREUVE ORALE

L'ÉPREUVE ÉCRITE

L'épreuve écrite a trois objectifs :

- évaluer votre aptitude à la compréhension écrite ;
- évaluer votre aptitude à l'expression écrite ;
- évaluer votre compétence linguistique.

Elle comporte différents types d'exercices dont le barème diffère selon les séries.

L'épreuve dure 3 heures dans les séries L, ES et S.
L'épreuve dure 2 heures dans les séries STT, STI, SMS et STL.

Dans les deux cas, réservez quinze minutes pour relire votre devoir.

RETENIR L'ESSENTIEL

Compréhension de l'écrit

Dans la série L, l'épreuve pourra porter sur un seul texte ou sur deux.

Dans toutes les autres séries, l'épreuve portera sur un seul texte (le même qu'en série L, ou une partie du texte de la série L, ou l'un des deux textes donnés à la série L).

Il s'agira d'extraits d'œuvres littéraires (nouvelle, roman, pièce de théâtre, essai...) ou d'articles de presse. Leur longueur totale n'excédera pas soixante lignes. Vous avez donc le temps de le(s) lire calmement en entier.

On pourra vous demander de prélever dans le texte, de reformuler, de justifier, de résumer, de répondre brièvement à des questions.

⚠️N'oubliez pas que les questions de compréhension comportent des indices qui vous aideront à comprendre et vous éviteront les fausses pistes.

Expression

Dans les séries S et ES et dans les séries STT, STI, SMS et STL, il s'agit d'expression semi-guidée et/ou d'expression libre. Les sujets seront liés ou non au texte de départ.

Vous devrez montrer que vous êtes capable de défendre un point de vue, d'exprimer un jugement, de commenter un fait de civilisation. Surveillez de très près dans cette partie de l'épreuve la correction de votre langage.

Compétence linguistique

Cette épreuve peut comporter par exemple des exercices de reformulation, de transposition, de transformation, d'imitation.

Dans la série L, LV1, la compétence linguistique n'est pas évaluée indépendamment de la compréhension et de l'expression. Elle peut donc s'intégrer au commentaire du texte par des questions sur sa construction, sur les procédés rhétoriques, sur la valeur des formes grammaticales.

Traduction

Le passage retenu pour la traduction en français ne dépassera pas dix lignes en série L.

En séries S et ES, on pourra vous demander de traduire cinq lignes. Il n'y a pas de traduction en séries STT, STI, SMS et STL.

⚠ *Pour la série L, LV1, compréhension, expression et compétence linguistique sont évaluées en bloc par un commentaire guidé (questions) ou par une discussion portant sur tout ou partie du texte. Seule la traduction est évaluée séparément.*

Quelques pièges et difficultés

■ Compréhension de l'écrit

Ne vous affolez pas si vous ignorez tel ou tel mot (cela ne vous empêchera pas de comprendre le texte dans son ensemble). Essayez de le décomposer, de le lire dans son contexte pour en déduire le sens.

174

Citer le texte signifie **choisir** la phrase ou le membre de phrase qui éclaire votre réponse. Ne citez que ce dont vous avez besoin pour l'étayer.

■ **Expression personnelle**

● *Expression semi-guidée*

« Semi-guidée » signifie que la consigne est d'utiliser certaines fonctions et certaines structures grammaticales.

Attention : exprimer le doute ne signifie pas employer le mot « doubt » mais utiliser des expressions fonctionnelles du doute (no one knows for sure…, to be likely to…, I don't understand why…).

● *Expression libre*

Lisez soigneusement les sujets. Ils peuvent comporter plusieurs questions.

Prenez le temps **de choisir le sujet** sur lequel vous pouvez le mieux vous exprimer (ce n'est pas automatiquement celui qui vous intéresse le plus) et **de faire un plan** (comme en français !), ce qui vous évitera d'écrire au fil de la plume… et de sortir du sujet.

Vous avez une certaine expérience du monde anglophone par la télévision, la musique, le cinéma, ou vos rencontres, vos voyages, vos lectures. N'hésitez pas à y faire référence **à condition qu'elle ait un rapport réel avec le sujet**.

■ **Compétence linguistique**

Lisez la consigne jusqu'au bout ! De cette façon, vous tiendrez compte de **tous** les éléments fournis.

Repérez le ou les points de grammaire sur le(s)quel(s) porte l'exercice.

Commencez par les exercices qui vous posent le moins de problèmes. Ne vous arrêtez pas sur une difficulté : vous y reviendrez plus tard.

■ **Traduction**

N'abordez la traduction qu'après vous être bien imprégné(e) du sens du texte dans son ensemble. Relisez plusieurs fois le passage retenu avant de commencer à le traduire.

Prenez garde à rester fidèle au sens du texte. On ne vous demande pas de l'interpréter mais de le traduire. Surveillez les temps employés. Repérez les faux amis.

Ne traduisez pas mot à mot, vous aboutiriez à une traduction artificielle, voire au contre-sens. Ne laissez pas de blancs, servez-vous du contexte pour donner au mot que vous ne connaissez pas un sens vraisemblable.

Ne laissez jamais le choix entre deux traductions. C'est à vous de choisir, pas au correcteur !

Veillez à la correction de votre français : il compte aussi dans la note finale !

Vous devrez, en série L, être sensible aux caractéristiques littéraires du texte : faites particulièrement attention aux niveaux de langue utilisés.

Notes

L'ÉPREUVE ORALE

L'épreuve orale comporte deux parties.

● Pour la première partie, l'examinateur choisit **un document de la liste** que vous lui présentez et vous demande de le commenter. Cette liste comporte un nombre variable de textes selon les séries. En série L, LV1 renforcée, un programme de lecture a été défini.

A ces textes, peuvent s'ajouter des documents iconographiques (et/ou audiovisuels en série L).

● Pour la deuxième partie, l'épreuve varie selon les séries.

Dans les séries L et ES, LV1 renforcée, elle peut porter sur un **document inconnu** (écrit, visuel, sonore ou audiovisuel).

Dans les autres séries, il s'agit d'un **entretien libre** avec l'examinateur. Vous devrez y manifester votre aptitude à réagir spontanément.

Dans tous les cas, la durée de la préparation et la durée de l'épreuve sont de vingt minutes.

RETENIR L'ESSENTIEL

Mener l'entretien

● **Pour commencer votre entretien**

Good morning. Good afternoon.
Here's (this is) the list of texts I've studied in class.

I think I'll start (begin) with...
I'd rather start (begin) with...
I'd like to start with...

Shall I read the text?
Shall I start from the beginning?

Would you like me to comment on the text now?
I'd like to comment on...

177

● **Si vous n'avez pas compris une question**

Could you please repeat the question?
Would you mind repeating the question?
Would you be so kind as to repeat the question?
Sorry (I'm afraid) I haven't understood your question.
I beg your pardon...
I'm not quite sure I understood your question (what you said)...

● **Pour terminer votre entretien**

Thank you (for listening to me).
Goodbye.

Construire votre commentaire

● **Commencer**

first, in the first place : *(tout) d'abord*
to begin with, for a start, as a starting point : *pour commencer*

● **Introduire une nouvelle idée**

secondly, in the second place : *deuxièmement*
then, next, afterwards : *puis, ensuite*
after insisting on : *après avoir insisté sur...*
moreover, furthermore, what is more, in addition to, besides : *de plus...*

● **Exprimer un balancement, une opposition**

on the one hand... on the other hand... : *d'une part... d'autre part...*
the former... the latter... : *le premier... le dernier...*

● **Reformuler**

in other words : *en d'autres termes*
in a nutshell (to put it in a nutshell) : *en deux mots*
that is to say, namely : *c'est-à-dire*
what I mean : *ce que je veux dire*   .

● **Exprimer votre opinion**

I share the author's viewpoint (point of view, opinion).
Je partage le point de vue de l'auteur.
I wonder whether... *Je me demande si...*

I think we mustn't go too far.
Je pense que nous ne devons pas aller trop loin.

Speaking for myself... *En ce qui me concerne...*

We are entitled to believe... *On a le droit de penser que...*

If we take into account... *Si nous tenons compte de...*

What is striking... *Ce qui me frappe...*

We can be impressed by the fact...
Nous pouvons être impressionnés par le fait...

It seems to me that... *Il me semble que...*

It may be argued that... *On peut avancer que...*

The point he makes here is quite relevant.
La remarque qu'il fait ici est tout à fait pertinente.

I am far from convinced that... *Je suis loin d'être convaincu(e) que...*

● **Replacer le document dans un contexte plus large**

It is linked to the problem of... It is related to the problem of...
Il est lié au problème de...

It brings out the problem of... *Cela soulève la question de...*

It questions (the American consumer society, the myth of the American dream).
Cela met en cause (la société de consommation américaine, le mythe du rêve américain).

● **Conclure**

lastly, finally : *enfin* (ne pas confondre avec "at last" qui exprime le soulagement)

to conclude (with), in conclusion, as a conclusion : *pour conclure*

in short : *en bref*

last but not least : *le dernier mais pas le moindre*

in the end : *à la fin*

to sum up : *pour résumer*

De nombreuse notions vous sont fournies
dans le chapitre : Pour s'exprimer de A à Z,
22 fiches d'expressions clés (p. 5 à 22).

Vous pouvez présenter vos commentaires dans l'ordre de votre choix.

Nous vous conseillons de préparer en premier lieu **le commentaire du texte étudié en classe**.

Cela doit être rapide : notez un plan et les idées directrices.

Si, en deuxième partie, vous devez commenter un texte inconnu, commencez par le lire en entier sans prendre de notes, pour en comprendre le sens général.

A la deuxième lecture, repérez les mots clés, les articulations du texte, pour commencer à construire votre commentaire.

● **Situer le texte**

It can be

a fictional text : *un texte de fiction,*

a passage from a novel : *un extrait d'un roman,*

a passage from a play : *un extrait d'une pièce de théâtre,*

a passage from a short story : *un extrait d'une nouvelle,*

a passage from a newspaper article : *un extrait d'article de journal,*

a criticism : *une critique,*

a poem : *un poème.*

It's a text by… *C'est un texte de…*

The text is taken from… *Le texte est tiré de…*

The scene takes place in that country, that town… *La scène se situe dans ce pays, cette ville…*

The date of the text is… *Ce texte date de…*

It takes place in the period when… *Il se situe à l'époque où…*

Ces éléments, qui concernent l'environnement du texte, seront souvent déterminants pour l'élaboration de votre commentaire.

- **Dégager les mots clés (keywords), les idées essentielles**

the main idea of the passage : *l'idée principale du passage*

a topic : *un sujet, un thème*

The text deals with, is about (et non pas "speaks of")...
Le texte traite de...

The text acquaints us with the problem of...
Ce texte nous informe sur le problème de...

The passage conveys an impression of...
Le passage donne une impression de...

The passage reveals, throws light on... *Le passage révèle, éclaire...*

The text aims at (+ V + ing)... *Le but du texte est de...*

The passage seems to suggest... *Le passage semble suggérer...*

The text can be divided into three main parts.
On peut distinguer trois parties principales.

The passage raises the question of... *Le passage soulève la question de...*

It's a story about...

The main themes, ideas are... *Les thèmes, les idées principales sont...*

- **Préciser le point de vue narratif**

The narrator is...

The writer speaks in the first person.

The story is told from the mother's viewpoint.

- **Désigner l'auteur**

the author, the writer : *l'auteur, l'écrivain*

the playwright : *l'auteur dramatique*

the novelist : *le romancier*

the critic : *le critique*

the poet : *le poète*

- **Définir les personnages**

The main characters are...

The relationships between the characters are...

- **Préciser les visées de l'auteur**

He describes, he gives a description of... *Il décrit...*
He meditates on... *Il réfléchit à...*
He presents us with... *Il nous présente...*
He raises the problem of... *Il soulève le problème de...*
He draws attention to... *Il attire l'attention sur...*
He insists on, emphasizes, stresses... *Il met l'accent sur...*
He examines, considers... *Il examine...*
He asserts that... *Il affirme que...*
He objects to... *Il proteste contre...*
His intention is to... *Son intention est de...*
He appeals to... *Il fait appel à...*
He criticizes... *Il critique....*
He analyzes... *Il analyse...*
He comments on (upon)... *Il commente...*
He denounces... *Il dénonce...*
He alludes to... *Il fait allusion à...*
He questions... *Il interroge...*
He expresses... *Il exprime...*
He aims at... *Il a pour but... Il vise...*

- **Définir ses moyens stylistiques**

The rhythm is lively. *Le rythme est vif.*
The rhythm is slow. *Le rythme est lent.*
The sentences are long. *Les phrases sont longues.*
The sentences are short, concise. *Les phrases sont courtes, concises.*
The style is repetitive. *Le style est répétitif.*
This word is repeated two, x times and this creates an atmosphere of...
Ce mot est répété deux, x fois et cela crée une atmosphère de...
These images, these metaphors create the impression that... *Ces images,
ces métaphores donnent l'impression que...*
The tone of this text is passionate. *Le ton de ce texte est passionné.*
The tone is sincere, affected. *Le ton est sincère, affecté.*
The tone is humoristic, comical, ironical. *Le ton est humoristique, comique,
ironique...*
The tone is poetical, lyrical. *Le ton est poétique, lyrique.*

- **Citer le texte**

As the writer puts it… *Comme le dit l'auteur…*

To quote the writer… *Pour citer l'auteur…*

a quotation : *une citation*

According to the author… *Selon l'auteur…*

we can pick out : ….

Le document iconographique

Si, en deuxième partie, vous devez commenter un document iconographique inconnu, laissez-vous tout d'abord imprégner par l'image, regardez-la sans idée préconçue.

- **Caractériser le document**

The document can be

a work of art : *une œuvre d'art,*

a painting : *un tableau,*

a drawing : *un dessin,*

a portrait : *un portrait,*

a sculpture : *une sculpture,*

a photograph : *une photographie,*

a cartoon (which often presents a caption) :
un dessin humoristique (qui comporte souvent une légende),

a comic strip composed of frames and balloons :
une bande dessinée composée de vignettes et de bulles,

an advertisement with or without a slogan :
une publicité avec ou sans slogan,

an extract from a film : *un extrait de film,*

a mural : *une fresque,*

graffiti : *des graffitis,*

a map : *une carte.*

The document is taken from a newspaper, a magazine, a book, a film.
Le document est extrait d'un journal, d'un magazine, d'un livre, d'un film.

183

● Décrire le document

Nous vous conseillons de partir d'une vue d'ensemble, d'une description générale pour en arriver à l'analyse des détails.

the setting : *le décor*

a close up : *un gros plan*

a long shot : *un plan d'ensemble*

in the foreground, in the background : *au premier plan, à l'arrière-plan*

in the distance : *au loin*

in the middle : *au milieu*

on the left, on the right : *à gauche, à droite*

at the top : *en haut*

at the bottom : *en bas*

in the top (upper) left hand corner : *en haut à gauche*

in the bottom (lower) left hand corner : *en bas à gauche*

● Exprimer un déplacement

forwards : *en avant*

backwards : *en arrière*

downwards : *vers le bas*

upwards : *vers le haut*

● Qualifier l'image

The picture is distinct. *L'image est nette.*

The picture is blurred. *L'image est floue.*

The picture is dark, light. *L'image est sombre, claire.*

The colours are bright, dull. *Les couleurs sont vives, ternes.*

● Where?

The scene takes place

in the outside : *à l'extérieur,*

in the country (country scenes),

in the city (street scenes),

in a garden,

by the seaside : *au bord de la mer,*

in a landscape : *dans un paysage,*

184

inside a house,

in an office,

in public places.

● When?

The picture gives clues about the time of the year...
L'image fournit des indices sur la période de l'année...

From the clothes, the landscape, I can guess the scene takes place in summer. *D'après les vêtements, le paysage, je peux supposer que la scène se déroule en été.*

● Who?

Pour décrire les personnages, mobilisez le vocabulaire relatif aux parties du corps, aux vêtements, aux attitudes *(postures)*.

He (she) looks old, young.

He (she) seems

happy,

anxious,

disappointed : *déçu(e)*,

surprised,

perplexed,

confident : *confiant(e)*,

worried : *soucieux(se)*,

sad : *triste*.

The characters are expressive, expressionless.
Les personnages sont expressifs, sans expression.

● Interpréter l'image

N'hésitez pas à émettre des hypothèses et même à construire une histoire autour de l'image et des personnages. Vous pourrez faire preuve d'un esprit de déduction et d'imagination.

What are they doing?

What were they doing before the photograph was taken?

What are they going to do?

What are they thinking about?

What might they say to each other?

What part of the society are they coming from?
What about their way of life?

- **Juger la qualité artistique, esthétique, l'humour, l'émotion du document**

Did the artist achieve his aim, reach his goal?
Is this advertisement convincing? *Cette publicité est-elle convaincante ?*
Is it effective? *Est-elle efficace ?*
Is this cartoon really funny?
Does it convey a message?

Le document sonore

Écoutez le document en entier sans chercher à prendre de notes.
Visez une compréhension globale du document, sans vous arrrêter à ce que vous ne comprenez pas.
Écoutez de nouveau l'enregistrement en retenant le maximum de renseignements. Au besoin, arrêtez le magnétophone pour prendre en notes les mots clés, les idées essentielles.
Utilisez les bruits de fond qui peuvent fournir des renseignements sur le passage, situez les personnages dans leur environnement.
Commencez à construire votre commentaire autour de grands axes.

- **Caractériser le document**

The document can be
a debate,
an interview,
a dialogue,
a speech,
an excerpt from a play or a film :
un extrait d'une pièce de théâtre ou d'un film,
a weather forecast : *un bulletin météo,*
an advertisement : *une publicité,*
the news : *les informations,*
an account : *un récit.*

186

● Who speaks?

a man, a woman, a child,

one character, several characters,

an anchorman (US), a newsreader (GB) : *un présentateur d'informations*,

an announcer : *un présentateur de radio ou de télévision*,

a politician,

a journalist,

a sports champion,

a musician,

an actor, an actress,

a housewife : *une femme au foyer*,

a playwright : *un auteur dramatique*.

● What about?

▓ Dégagez les idées générales, les mots clés *(keywords)*.

The person speaks of a tournament. *La personne parle d'un tournoi.*
She tells us...

He debates about a strike. *Il discute d'une grève.*

She describes a crime. *Elle décrit un crime.*

She comments on (upon) the elections. *Elle commente les élections.*

He criticizes...

He denounces...

We are told that... *On nous dit que...*

We are given some information about... *On nous donne des informations sur...*

This document is fictional. *C'est un document de fiction.*

The document is non fictional. *Il s'agit de faits réels.*

▌ Situez le document dans le temps en essayant de le lier à des faits
▌ de civilisation ou à des événements connus.

● Caractériser les personnages

The characters can have a foreign accent.

The characters may be convincing.
Les personnages peuvent être convaincants.

They may be

persuasive,
objective,
sad, gloomy : *tristes,*
amusing : *amusants,*
cheerful : *gais,*
biased, prejudiced : *partiaux.*

The voice can be

audible : *perceptible,*
sharp : *aiguë,*
muffled : *étouffée.*

The characters speak in a loud voice, in a low voice.
Les personnages parlent fort, parlent à voix basse.
They whisper. *Ils murmurent.*
They scream, they shout. *Ils crient.*
They stammer. *Ils bégayent.*

● Décrire les bruits de fond

I can hear a knock, a ring at the door.
J'entends quelqu'un qui frappe, qui sonne à la porte.
I can hear a scream, a shot. *J'entends un cri, un coup de feu.*
A dog barks. *Un chien aboie.*
Somebody snores. *Quelqu'un ronfle.*
Somebody sneezes. *Quelqu'un éternue.*
A door creaks. *Une porte craque.*
A door bangs. *Une porte claque.*
A telephone rings. *Un téléphone sonne.*
A crash is heard. *On entend un fracas.*
We hear the roar of a car engine.
On entend le vrombissement d'un moteur de voiture.
Someone is laughing, crying. *Quelqu'un rit, pleure.*

● **Définir le langage utilisé**

The speech level *(niveau de langue)* can be

sophisticated,
formal : *soigné,*
colloquial : *familier.*

The characters use slang words.
Les personnages emploient des mots d'argot.

The sentences can be long, short, complex.

The style can be

clear,
plain : *simple,*
elaborate : *recherché,*
lyrical,
lively : *vivant* ⇐
confused : *confus,*
accurate : *précis,*
refined : *raffiné,*
pedantic : *pédant,*
comical,
repetitive.

Quelques pièges et difficultés

■ Le document écrit

Au cours de la première partie, on pourra vous demander de **lire le texte** : entraînez-vous tout au long de l'année afin d'éviter une lecture monotone et incorrecte. Repérez les accents toniques, imprégnez-vous du rythme de l'écriture. Pensez que la lecture permet à l'examinateur d'évaluer votre compréhension du texte.

On pourra vous demander de **traduire quelques lignes**. Ne vous inquiétez pas : l'examinateur peut chercher ainsi à vous faire parler d'un aspect du texte que vous avez négligé jusque-là.

Si vous êtes interrogé sur une **œuvre complète**, vous devrez en présenter le contenu (action, personnages, contexte, thèmes) et porter un jugement personnel. N'apprenez rien par cœur, ni présentation, ni résumé. Votre examinateur vous évalue sur vos capacités de réaction spontanée, non sur le bachotage.

Ne rédigez pas votre commentaire complètement. Notez seulement le plan et les idées directrices.

■ Le document iconographique

Prenez le temps de lire l'image. Différenciez le général et les points de détail. Relevez les éléments significatifs.

Mobilisez vos connaissances grammaticales : prépositions exprimant le lieu, verbes de mouvement, expression de la probabilité (au moment des hypothèses d'interprétation).

■ Le document sonore

Ne vous découragez pas si certains mots vous échappent. Concentrez-vous sur ce que vous comprenez.

Utilisez les bruits de fond (pour lesquels vous n'avez besoin d'aucun dictionnaire !) pour vous représenter la situation, caractériser l'ambiance du document.

Si vous ne comprenez que peu de choses, ce n'est pas dramatique. Concentrez-vous sur un ou deux mots clés que vous avez réussi à dégager du document et fondez sur eux votre commentaire. L'épreuve vise en grande partie à juger la manière dont vous vous exprimez. Vous pouvez donc montrer vos compétences sans maîtriser tout le document.